The Book of Jessica

The Book of Jessica

A Theatrical Transformation

Linda Griffiths & Maria Campbell

The Coach House Press Toronto

Jessica is fully protected by copyright. All enquiries
concerning performing rights, professional or
amateur, readings, or any other use of this material
should be directed to:

Great North Artists Management, Inc.
350 Dupont Street
Toronto, Ontario, Canada M5R 1V9

Published with the generous assistance of
the Canada Council, the Ontario Arts Council,
and the Ontario Ministry of Culture and Communications.

Cover photo: Paul Orenstein
Text design: Nelson Adams

THIRD PRINTING

Canadian Cataloguing in Publication Data

Griffiths, Linda, 1956-
The Book of Jessica

ISBN 0-88910-380-1

I. Campbell, Maria. II. Griffiths, Linda, 1956-
III. Title.

PS8563.R536B6 1989   C812 '.54   C89-094808-911
PR9199.3.G75B6 1989

*To my son Daniel, who has given
me encouragement, support and
sometimes light in my search for
mother and grandmother.*

Maria

*To the sisters who have
helped me through:
Linda, Nicki, and Clare.*

Linda

And to Paul, for the process.

Linda and Maria

Contents

History

Winter 1974, Edmonton. Maria Campbell sees Clarke Roger's production of *Almighty Voice,* and decides she wants to do theatre.

Fall 1976, Saskatoon. Paul Thompson, artistic director of Theatre Passe Muraille, tours with *The West Show.* Maria and Paul connect and discuss doing a project together.

Summer 1979, Edmonton. Paul directs an improvisational workshop with Maria. Initial exploration occurs.

Winter 1980, Edmonton. On Paul's suggestion, Maria meets Linda Griffiths, on tour with her one-person show, *Maggie & Pierre.* They decide that Linda will improvise and perform the central character in a story as yet unformed.

Spring 1982, Regina. Maria and Linda drive through Saskatchewan and Alberta in Maria's old station wagon. Research stage.

July 1982, Edmonton. First full-scale improvisational jam session. Paul directs, Maria feeds in material, Linda plays Jessica. Actors are Tantoo Cardinal, Graham Greene, Bob Bainborough.

August 1982, Toronto. Linda, Paul and Maria meet in the Backspace at Theatre Passe Muraille. Linda improvises the play, with Maria and Paul feeding in.

September 1982, Saskatoon. Paul, Maria and Linda piece together the transcribed improvisations from the Toronto session into a script.

October – November 1982, Saskatoon. The show is rehearsed and performed at 25th Street House Theatre. It has a successful run, but ends in disagreement.

1982 – 1985, Toronto – Saskatoon. There is no contact between Maria and Paul or Linda. Silence on the project.

March 1985, Toronto. Linda rewrites and restructures *Jessica.*

April 1985, Toronto. Clarke Rogers, now artistic director of Theatre Passe Muraille, begins dramaturgy on the new script.

June 1985, Toronto – Batoche. Linda sends Maria the new script. Maria is angry.

August 1985, Batoche. Paul Thompson and Clarke Rogers visit Maria during the Metis celebration, 'Back to Batoche.' Maria agrees to meet with Linda to discuss *Jessica.*

September 1985, Batoche. Linda visits Maria at The Crossing

(Gabriel Dumont's homestead). Maria gives suggestions and comments, and suggests they direct the new production of *Jessica* together.

October–November 1985, Toronto. Linda rewrites *Jessica* again.

January – February 1986, Toronto. At the last moment, Maria is unable to go to Toronto to co-direct *Jessica*. Linda casts the play and begins directing. Clarke Rogers takes over as co-director. *Jessica* opens at Theatre Passe Muraille, and is well received.

April – May 1986, Toronto. *Jessica* wins the Dora Mavor Moore Award for Outstanding New Play. *Jessica* is a runner-up for the Chalmers Award. *Jessica* plays at the Quinzanne International Festival in Quebec City, and wins as Best Canadian Production.

July 1986, Batoche. Linda visits Maria to discuss the publication of *Jessica*. Maria suggests that they instead write a book of the story of the making of the play, which would include the playscript. Linda agrees.

January 1987, Toronto – Saskatoon. This new idea now appears impossible. Linda writes her version of the story but is dissatisfied. Maria pulls out notes and writings but assemblage is difficult.

January 1988, Saskatoon. Linda visits Maria. They begin talking more frankly about their time together. Linda starts writing down their conversations on computer.

June 1988, Toronto. Maria visits Linda. They again try writing the story, but are dissatisfied. Finally, they begin taping their conversations about *Jessica*.

November 1988, Toronto – Saskatoon. Individually, Maria and Linda go through two hundred and fifty pages of transcribed tape. Publication deadline is March 1, 1989.

January 1989, Toronto. Linda begins editing the tapes. Maria plans to join her later in January to work on structure and editing.

January 1989, Toronto – Saskatoon. Maria announces her intention to run for President of the Metis Society of Saskatchewan. Her schedule makes further work on the book impossible. Linda's contribution to her campaign is the editing and structuring of this book ... the red cloth.

Spiritual Things

I thought it was over. Inside I knew better, but on the surface, I thought it was over. *Jessica* would be published, and that would be it. The most I had to do was figure out the stage directions. But when I talked to Maria, she said, 'There's all kinds of stuff around the play that isn't in the play. There's the whole story of what happened to both of us, we should put it all in the book. Who reads plays, anyway?' I felt that familiar arrowhead point in the pit of my stomach.

MARIA   She came out to talk about that damn play, she wants to have it published. She's all crippled up from whatever happened and I still feel like some Siamese twin with her. I want her to go away, to leave me alone, but we're by the river at The Crossing and she's dipping her toes in the water and I hear myself saying, 'Let's tell the story of what happened, if we do that then maybe we'll be free of the whole thing, heal everything.' And I kick myself, 'What did I just say? Who could stand to open it all again? Am I crazy?'

Open it all up again? And it started to come back, the strangeness of that time, the feeling of being exposed, small and white, stretching myself so that my brain was bursting, being told, 'It's not your brain where it has to come from.' Being warped into another woman's frame of mind, frame of context, feeling some kind of connection with her, the spookiness of it all. It's still spooky, after all this time.

I want to write about 'her'. A 'her' who was an actress and an improvisor and a kind of adventurer who stumbled into something more profound, more terrifying, more personal and more political than anything she ever wanted to know. But she did want to know, badly enough to....

I did all kinds of things, impersonated the Prime Minister, improvised, wrote, acted, a real theatrical junkie. I had some kind of connection with the spirits, we called them 'the theatre gods,' and whether it was Pan or Bacchus or a chorus of lesser and greater muses, it didn't matter, you were just supposed to feel them. For years I worked in Paul Thompson's version of collective theatre,

combining politics, sociology and a strange robust kind of patrio-
tism, 'grounding' he called it. His rehearsal process was a kind of
automatic energy exchange that defied logical description. The
shows were grounded by a subject, any subject, sometimes a community of farmers, sometimes forgotten history, sometimes the
tenor of the land itself. The 'subject' was researched to the utmost,
the actors using real personalities as the basis for characters, everything had to be rooted in a reality you could touch. Then reality got
thrown out the window to the actor's imagination. Vaguely, all this
was fueled by something called 'the energies.'

I liked to climb inside other people's psyches and kind of ... sibyl
them. I was taught that you could open yourself to anything, anyone, let the energy pour through you, and something would happen. I was ravenous for those moments. But the 'subject' was never
in the room, never a part of the process, until *Jessica*. Then the old,
half-digested, theatrical gods met Maria and her Native spirits, and
all hell broke loose.

MARIA Don't you remember the time I tried to hit you with my
cowboy boots?

LINDA What?

MARIA The time I got so mad at you I was going to hit you with those
cowboy boots and Tantoo had to drag me away and calm me
down outside.

LINDA No, I don't remember.

MARIA You don't? I've been feeling bad about that for five years, I felt
so bad I gave Paul those boots.

LINDA You're kidding. Is that why you gave him those boots? He
wore them all the time for months.

MARIA Yeah, that's why I gave them away, then I freaked out and....

That's all part of the fun of it, but there's a tantrum I have to have,
the one I never had, not out loud.

LINDA I'm still not over it, I'll never be over it, that was the hardest,
the scariest, the most lost time. Nobody approved of me, even
though I worked my guts out. I worked and worked, and
invented and wove, and all they could do was ask for more
and tell me I wasn't jumping off the cliff. I opened myself to
the spirits of Native people, and then warred with my own,
and meanwhile there was a play to do. But I was wrong,

always wrong, because I was white and didn't know anything, but that was the point, that's what they asked me to do. There's never been a crash course like that, never, not one that demands a result. And still they were mad at me for something I couldn't help. But I stood there in front of them, with someone else's bad dreams, and my own, and I still did it!

MARIA She always looked like the Virgin Mary, passive, a blank look in her eyes, smiling, she never stopped smiling, smiled so much I just wanted to smack her and smack her so she'd stop that smiling. I talked to her and talked to her, I didn't want her to feel sorry for herself, I didn't want her to feel sorry for me. She walked around like a missionary, begging for something with one hand – give it to me, tell me about it – just bleeding all of me dry. She made me think of those stupid stories in the *National Enquirer*: 'Virgin Mary Bleeds as Visitors Watch in Horror.'

I used to expect her to begin oozing blood while we were in rehearsals, because there was nothing else coming out. She wanted to suffer like I had suffered, but how did she know what I'd suffered, of if I'd suffered? Then she'd take it all. When I started to feel sorry for her, thinking, 'She's smiling because she's hurting, and she's bleeding because of the hurt,' then I'd see my mother in her, my mother kneeling in front of this statue. A statue with white skin, and black hair, and empty blue eyes, and then she and my mother and the Virgin Mary would merge. I'd want to take her, and hold her, and rock her, and sing songs to her, I wanted to heal her. Everytime I'd feel like that, she'd jump on the stage and she'd play it all back, and I'd stand there feeling like she'd stolen my thoughts. She'd just take it all.

The Beginning

I was white. Really white. Whether white is a sensibility or a colour, sometimes it can be a place. All the traveling, all the danger, all the wildness of theatre life had never really touched that place. Maybe that's bullshit. The west had touched it. The first view of the prairie had touched it. Cowboy boots had touched it, and drinking draft beer in beer parlours had definitely smudged things a bit, and the first view of Indians walking five strong down Twentieth Street had been something in the order of a different feeling.

So many ties, threads, connections, personalities and history had gone into the idea of doing *Jessica* that no one knew where it had started. Ten years before, Clarke Rogers had directed a production called *Almighty Voice*. This had been created and performed by white actors.

MARIA I didn't know much about theatre, but I was doing community work when I saw *Almighty Voice*. I went to the play because the Native comunity was in an uproar. It was a play about Native people done by whites; it also delved into a spiritual world that we felt should be interpreted by Natives themselves. I went to denounce it, and ended up defending it.

In that production of *Almighty Voice* I saw something really powerful happen, something that educated, that healed, that empowered people; it was fun and it was magical. It was a play that could be performed in a back alley, in a community hall or in a clearing in the bush. I talked with Clarke Rogers and he understood our need to take this kind of power to the communities.

I was desperate for skills and tools to help make change. I started going to libraries finding books that were about theatre. I and several other women tried to write a play using these books as a guideline. It didn't work.

Then Paul Thompson came to town with *The West Show*. Everybody was buzzing, he was the founder of Theatre Passe Muraille, a free theatre that nurtured and encouraged the kinds of things we were trying to do. I met him and a new door opened for me. His energy was incredible, it made my head work and I felt like I was flying, like there was no such thing as impossible. I've never met anyone like him since. My weird world appeared normal to him, so I talked and talked. We'd do a play together – no, he couldn't teach me what he knew, but that was okay, I was never a good student. Instead, we'd exchange. I'd learn from taking part in 'the process,' and in return I'd give my bag of goodness knows what. The play would be about being a woman and the struggle of trying to understand what that meant. 'Jessica' came later, from a Waylon Jennings song, 'Ladies Love Outlaws.'

In the discussion after *Almighty Voice*, Maria argued that no one can own the spiritual power in a culture, that by its nature it must be open to everyone. She also argued, as she did during *Jessica*, that many Native people have white blood, so how could they shut out whites who really wanted to learn?

MARIA   God, if she only knew. If she only knew how many times I wanted to tell her, 'Just take all your stuff and get out, you're white, you have no business here, I don't know why I invited you, I don't know why I ever thought that spiritual power was for both of us, go find your own spirits, your own power.' But every time I started to do that, I'd see a circle of grandmothers and the circle of grandmothers had no colour.

Then Paul Thompson connected with Maria, for years discussing developing a theatrical production with her. Paul and Maria wanted the project to deal directly with the spiritual world.

MARIA   What is she talking about anyway? This was not supposed to be a play about spiritual worlds, it was supposed to be a play about a woman struggling with two cultures, and how she got them balanced; because when she leaned into one, a part of her got lost, so she had to lean into the other one and try to understand and find a balance.

   Spirits were in both those cultures, but this whole thing about 'spirits' and all this whooey-whooey stuff was enough to scare the pants off me. I got so scared sometimes, I couldn't go outside at night during rehearsals. When I had talked about doing a play with Paul we talked about the prairie, the dancing, the smells, about prairie things. We didn't talk that much about spirits, this level and that level, then all of a sudden we were into spiritual power. That's why I hate working with the English language, and why I have a hard time working with white people, because everything means something else. 'Spiritual power my ass,' I thought, 'Wait till they find out I don't have any power.'

Finally, I was part of the idea, about to work with Paul Thompson, director of the maverick Theatre Passe Muraille, and Maria Campbell, Metis writer, activist, teacher, catalyst....

MARIA What a bunch of garbage. I'm a community worker. A mom.
'Metis writer'? – I should have a giant typewriter? 'Activist'?
– I should be throwing Molotov cocktails? It just sounds so ...
so much like a white professor introducing me at a
convention of anthropologists.

No one even knew what the idea was exactly. Something to do with spiritual things. Something to do with Native people. Mixed-blood people. Something to do with women. A woman. Something springing from the west.

If there was earth, air, fire and water, only one of these forces really made sense to me. I'd always felt as if I was ninety-five percent air. Sometimes hot air. One of the many things that made me hungry for this project was that I knew it would have everything to do with the earth. I was as prepared on the theatre side as I could be, or so I thought.

After I'd been kicked out of theatre school, I'd briefly gone into teaching, working in 'inner-city schools,' which meant schools in Montreal slums.

I decided to do a whole project about Native people. I screened a film about the buffalo hunt for my fifth-grade students, thinking it would be a treat for them. The only trouble was, I'd screened it in a bright room, not seeing it clearly. The kids were ready, and the film started. It began with an endless shot of a buffalo with testicles the size of basketballs, and a grossly enlarged penis that actually bounced on the prairie as he ran. The first kid pointed, then the next, the girls started squealing, the boys howling, there was mayhem, and still that buffalo pounded his way at the head of the herd. It seemed to go on forever. I had to stop the film. All my careful preparation about 'The Wrongs Done Our Native Peoples' was undone. It was as if the buffalo got the last laugh.

Then there was a picture I had never forgotten. Some white man with a camera had snuck into one of the last Native Sun Dance ceremonies. In a huge exposure I saw the face of a man, with bones stuck through his chest, tied to ropes attached to a central pole. He was pulling against the ropes, angled backwards, so the bones would be torn free of the flesh. His neck was straight and tall right up from his spine. There is no describing the look on his face, but it burned right through me.

MARIA You sure never forgot it, you carried that look around for
       months, any chance to suffer, you were willing to take lessons.
LINDA That's an easy shot.

I had two months to think about the project and read books. Then I
met her. There's something frightening about theatrical confi-
dence, it knows no bounds.

The woman in the restaurant was quiet and dignified, almost
strangely so. I don't know what I expected, but she wasn't what I
expected. She had the kind of energy that turned me into an enthu-
siastic cheerleader, full of excited questions and a terror of silence.
Yet, as we spoke, something was happening. The electricity was
strong, we were both racing with the contact.

MARIA She didn't know that I was totally freaked out by her, I was
       scared to open my mouth for fear I'd say something stupid.
       What did I know about theatre? I mean, this woman was a
       star. Not only was she an actress, but according to Paul she
       was one of the best improvisors in the country. Never mind
       that I didn't know exactly what 'improvise' meant, it sounded
       really important. When I think of her thinking of me as
       dignified and quiet, it sounds so romantic, a teacher should be
       dignified and quiet. I wonder how many people know it's just
       better sometimes to be quiet for fear you'll appear the fool.

Maria had written a best-selling book called *Halfbreed*, which was
essentially the story of her life. But that was ten years ago. This pro-
posed play was not to be an adaptation of the book, but was to
explore what had happened to her since its publication. She said
she believed that mixed-blood people were the obvious link
between whites and Natives, and that they would be the ones to
bring about a renaissance in spiritual thought. Under Paul's guid-
ance, we were to make up a woman who was Maria, but not really. I
would hear parts of the book not included in the published version,
I would hear stories. The stories included her re-entry into a Native
spiritual world. I would become Maria, or a version of Maria. I
would interpret the world she showed me. Then, somehow, there
would be a play.

MARIA I told her I'd always felt a kind of historical guilt because we
       had been (when I say 'we,' I mean Metis people, Halfbreed

people, mixed-blood people) the link between Indians and whites. We had acted as interpreters in treaties, we had walked ahead of the explorers and showed them the way. In the course of trying to deal with that guilt, I had come to the realization, on both sides, that it wasn't my guilt. That garbage belonged to both those two peoples, not to my people. We were children of two peoples who wanted something of each other. And when they started to hate each other, they focused that hate on us, their children, until we were just like a band of gypsies moving around, landless, carrying the few things that they had cast off – a little bit of a language, a little bit of culture. And part of my own journey had forced me to look at all the stuff that I had put in this packsack that I was carrying around with me and try and find a way to sort it all out; try and replace the negative with things from both peoples that were precious and beautiful; and to look at what we had done. We had created a new culture and built a new nation.

And I looked all over, traveled all over, finally went home after many years. The writing of *Halfbreed* was part of that journey home. I found it there, in the spirituality of my own people. Their ability to laugh, to dance, to celebrate something as basic as life.

My first teacher was a Halfbreed woman. She was the one who taught me that the earth was my mother, and made me fanatical about searching her out. She made me look into my Indian side, and there I found it. But I had to dig through a lot of stuff because they said 'Mother,' but there was no real connection to her, it was only the 'Father,' the 'Grandfathers' that have the power; the influence of Christianity had pushed her out and the white side didn't even say 'Mother' anymore. But this teacher told me that once, a long time ago, we all had 'Mother,' and that we were unbalanced because we could no longer revere her.

The Station Wagon

A year later, Maria and I were in a station wagon going north. We drove through endless stretches of bush. Solid, relentless, smokey green on either side of us, for hours.

Even those first few days, the gap between Maria and I widened at times to a gulf that seemed impassable. I had to find a way to ask the most personal questions. She had to find a way to reveal things to me. My gung-ho energy began to fade a little. It was hard to pump a complete stranger without turning into an idiot or a journalist. 'Stuff me, inject me,' I wanted to say, 'Make me understand and I'll make an audience understand.' Eighteen years separated us, as well as race, class, culture, social work, political work, and, in its own category, what Maria called 'the street' – almost every boundary I knew, and lots I didn't know.

MARIA How do you tell the Virgin Mary about things you've done that you don't even want to think about yourself? It was really easy to tell her about my people's history, about the politics, the organizing, the oppression. It was easy to tell her about the anger and the hate I was trying to work through. But how could I tell her about the things that I didn't even want to admit to myself? I could tell her about the men, the drugs, the pain, all of it. But the underlying stuff.... How do you tell the Virgin Mary that your dream is to rip down all the foundations of Christiantity when she is the entrance to that world?

We turned down a dirt road, and the bush opened up into a kind of sand pit, almost like a settlement, with a few trailers, stuck at odd angles. In one of them was a classic Metis man with black curly hair, white teeth and startling blue eyes. He was Maria's brother.

Maria wanted me to meet her family, her world. I brushed sand out of the trailer, I awkwardly carried water to wash dishes, I sat in the kitchen with four other women in complete silence, drinking tea. It was the silences that made me feel white. I wanted to say, 'All right, let's get a real conversation going here.' I got the feeling that communication was happening, but I couldn't tell what it was. I ended up with a constant half smile on my face, trying to catch the jokes before they were made. Or maybe they weren't made, just thought. I felt disconnected, as if I had huge white hands dangling from a body not standing on the ground.

Maria was to speak at a graduation of Native teachers. There was to be a dance afterwards. When Maria saw my attempt at an outfit, she said, 'You can't wear that, people will think you're poor and feel sorry for you.' I didn't know what to say. Finally I wore a wide pink skirt, a white lace top, brushed hair and ankle socks.

I always liked to look a little offbeat, but now I was the girl my mother wanted me to be. I couldn't have looked whiter. But maybe not. My mother's Nova Scotian clan had black hair and blue eyes, the 'Black Scots,' they were called. As I stood beside Maria, I thought, 'I could be one of her daughters.'

MARIA I thought that too. When I started taking her into the communities, I thought, 'She could be one of my daughters.'

The ceremony was in a gymnasium with the inevitable basketball net hanging directly over the speakers' heads. Here were quiet, conservatively dressed people sitting in rows. Where was the exoticism of the books I'd been reading? When would the chanting start? I saw the other white people and I didn't want to be one of them.

As Maria rose to speak, I sensed a change in the room. Hard to say what it was, it was as if the air thickened, or the tinny echo from the cinderblocked walls softened, or the dressed-up stiffness of the crowd relaxed. Something changed. She changed with it. She spoke with a tiny voice and a bowed head. The whole audience knew her.

At the end of her speech I rose to my feet with the rest of the crowd, fighting back tears, with a giant lump in my throat. She told the truth about what it was to be a Native child, taught by white teachers who penalized them for their very culture. Guilt hit me like a club. Why had these people had so much trouble? Because of me. Because of the oppressive behavior of my people. Who were 'my people?'

The lights dimmed, the chairs were cleared, and the band began to play. We all sat at a table – Maria, her brother, his wife, and some other people I didn't know. I felt very young, as if I were at a dance with my parents, something I had never done. Everything was separated in my world, but here everything was mixed – old people, parents, adolescents, children.

Grateful for the pink skirt, I relaxed and was asked to dance. But it was the fiddle music that did it. People began step-dancing in circles, feet jumping and pounding, arms limp to their sides. Something stirred my blood in a familiar way. My feet couldn't keep still. It was the demon fiddler, who was Scots, who was Irish, who was French, who was Cree. I saw pictures of wind-swept moors, heard the ocean, felt the desire to run screaming down hills with a standard in my hand. Soon it was time to leave, and the group rose from the table, but the fiddler was too strong. I began to dance all by myself at the edge of the crowd, as Maria and her family watched and laughed. People were watching, but I didn't care. I was no longer the oppressor, I danced away the oppressor.

MARIA She was a good dancer. That was the first time I started to accept her; she didn't get up to dance for any man, to cozy up to them, like most of the white women who come to our community and see dancing with some wild Halfbreed guy as a way in. Instead, she danced and made us feel like she was our family, one of us. We all felt that we wanted to cheer her on. It was like the first time I saw my kids get up and dance, in front of the old people, who always watched. It makes you feel like you want to start clapping, it's like tuning into somebody. When she was dancing, I felt, 'Yeah, I can talk to her, she hears the same music that I hear.'

I remember when you came out the next morning and everyone was sitting out front. A whole bunch of people had come over, they were celebrating, you'd made them happy. And you were so embarrassed, you practically crossed your legs around themselves, you blushed and wrang your hands, like a colt. But the really important thing was that your eyes were bright and flashing and when somebody would say something, you were flashing back. It wasn't the way an outsider looks at our people. You were flirting, it was like you were still dancing. Halfbreed people flirt a lot, not like they want to come onto you, but like there's so much in the world to be happy about.

It was very possible I'd just made an ass of myself. That's what I thought when I woke up in the trailer the next morning.

The crash course continued. I had homework. The books Maria suggested seemed to have nothing to do with Indians or Native spirituality. They gave me the feeling I was doing something wrong, something ... almost blasphemous. Yet they were exciting, spoke of things I had imagined alone in my room at twelve years old, then crushed because there was no place for those thoughts in the real world. They spoke of a goddess. They spoke of witch burnings and Babylon, of ecstacy and lunacy and the moon. Earth Mother, moons, circles, spirals, great sows devouring children, druids performed rituals, horned gods appeared at night.

They spoke of faerie tales and dreams. They blasted open my Catholic upbringing, my avoidance of religious thought, allowing me to give some value to what I had been taught. In my world, religion was a thing to be avoided, a right-wing place that chained sexuality and freedom to guilt. Yet I used to like the silent moments in church, when we weren't speaking about sins, when we just prayed. It was part of me, this idea of prayer.

We drove and drove, the two of us locked in the brown station wagon. I wanted to get to the 'street' part, but I didn't know how to broach the subject. Suddenly I was polite in a way I hadn't been in years. I couldn't find a way to say, 'So how did you start hooking?', or, 'What's it like to be strung out on smack?' At least not to a stranger. Maria's experiences were a little different from mine. Like, totally different. Underneath the questions and answers, I knew there was a pressure cooker of a woman beside me. She might get mad. She might stop the car and tell me to get out. She might turn on me in some way if I did the wrong thing, said the wrong thing, and yet she was explaining intimate details of her story to me with exemplary patience. I was doing research like the good improvisational animal I had become. I got through to Pierre Trudeau, I would get through to Maria.

'So how did you start, uhh, get into ... become ... how did the prostitution thing ... what was it like?' She didn't hesitate, and the strangeness of the way she spoke, was the maternity of it.

As she took me into her past, I watched her transform, saw the blue jeans become silk stockings, saw the demure tilt of her head. I soon would sit like this, speak like this. I breathed her in without thinking.

Faust

We were now traveling northwest, to visit Maria's friend and teacher, Hannah. When we finally arrived at the tiny town, a rusted sign read, 'Faust.' I was learning about the spirits' sense of humour. A little twisted.

Again we were in a trailer, this time a big one with all the conveniences. Hannah was a nut-like woman, five-feet tall and two-feet wide, with a black braid down her back. She was younger than I expected, and funnier, with a crazy cracked laugh and plump arms that waved around when she spoke. Once more, seemingly silent women cooked, cleaned and relaxed in the glowing Simpson-Sears catologue living room. I knew Hannah had been told something of the project, that's all I knew.

Again I found myself reduced to a younger, ghost-like self. Hannah zeroed in on me. Part of her routine was to razz Maria for not following more traditional ways, not helping her perform the ceremonies, for remaining in the city and not living close to the land. Hannah tried to impress on me the importance of these things, as Maria laughed and answered back. They were good together.

MARIA   When I brought you there the first time, she was upset, I mean, she was mad.

LINDA   For bringing me?

MARIA   Because she knew I was going to do this play, and she kept telling me, 'Don't do it. You are going to be putting stuff out there that nobody's got any business knowing about.' Hannah is an absolute hard-core traditionalist. She is as traditional as a Catholic priest, only on the other extreme.

'You are not ready to start talking to anybody about that stuff.' 'I know,' I'd say, 'but I'm an artist, I'm not a teacher, I'm not trying to teach anybody.' 'Yes, you are, you are trying to teach people stuff.' 'I'm not trying to teach them anything. I'm trying to put something on stage, so that other people won't be so lost.' She was absolutely against it, so I didn't let her know we were coming, because the only way that I could get you to understand my relationship with her was for you to see me with her.

In the back of my head, just like you did when you started to rewrite the play, I thought that she wouldn't demolish me because there was too much between us. But I still went there believing that she would do something to you in that ceremony, something to absolutely scare the shit out of you.

All the time that you and I were sitting in that room, she was throwing balls of energy at me. She'd never done that before, and I'm using 'energy' for lack of a better word. Oh, she'd given me little jolts before, but never like she was doing that day. They were coming so fast and hard that I felt like I was going to explode. That was happening while we were sitting there drinking tea, talking, laughing, joking, while she was telling you those stories.

I was terrified, but I knew I was going to do the play anyway. You know what I mean. Like what you're telling me about writing *Jessica*. 'I've got to have your blessing, but I'm going to do it anyway, with or without the blessing.'

We have always had a great, but strange, relationship. She teaches me by scaring the hell out of me, that's what happened that day. I'd always been afraid of her ... no, not her, but ... well ... her power. Is that a good word? The only way I've ever been able to move forward in my life is to look at what I'm afraid of. You know, look fear in the face. Once I do that I can go on, and she knew that long before I did. I wanted to do the play, so I got brave enough to give some of the energy she was throwing at me back to her. The last jolt she gave me almost paralyzed me, but I reacted. For the first time in my relationship with her I sent it back. I had to before going into that ceremony. She got it, and laughed....

LINDA   Yeah?

MARIA   Then I felt like, 'Yeah, I'm okay, my insides tell me I'm okay.' But if I hadn't been able to shoot it back to her, we would have ran home. At that point, I knew I was going to do the play. And I knew I wasn't afraid of her anymore. It doesn't mean that she still won't zap me, but the fear that I had of her, for probably about ten years, was gone. And I knew, when I went into that ceremony, that even if she were to do something, you were going to be okay. I would be able to look after you.

The ceremony that night was the end of a weekend healing. A bunch of us went over to an empty farmhouse beside the trailer with sleeping bags, blankets, hammers and nails. I was so happy to be doing something, anything but trying to fit in, that I didn't question what it was we were doing. We spread the blankets and sleeping bags over the windows of the second floor of the farmhouse and nailed them in place. Sometimes two or three blankets were used for one window. We could still see clearly though, it was a sunny summer day.

Back at the trailer, the women were getting a spread of food ready. We would eat after the ceremony. I caught sight of Maria massaging Hannah's back before we went in.

The women changed into skirts. By this time the sun had set. Maria and I walked across the grass, looking up at a northern sky.

I tried to remember the things she had told me, how to sit, how to watch, how to pray. We were the last to enter the farmhouse, I was excited and nervous, but totally unprepared for the sight that greeted me as I mounted the stairs.

Time warped, smell warped, sight warped. It was the smell that overpowered me at first, the smell of sweet grass burning in a closed room. An ancient kind of smell, dark, a smell to lift the senses, unlock the heart and mind. A smell that makes you want to be true to yourself. I nearly fell down the stairs as it hit me. There was smoke in the air, and the only light was flame.

Lined up against the wall of a room that was the entire second story, were about twenty Native people – men, women, children, talking quietly and waiting to begin. They were utterly different from the awkwardly modern people who had eaten lunch, nailed up blankets and hung around quietly in the afternoon shade. They were now what I imagined 'Native' to be. They were powerful, about to be in the presence of the spirits.

The faces watched me without curiosity as I found my place against the wall, clinging to Maria as much as I could. The disorientation of time was so strong that everyone in the room seemed to be in costume. It occurred to me that I had no idea what was going to happen; my reading, my piles of books, were meaningless and dry. In the middle of the room, spread out on a large cloth were objects of power, bundles of cloth, pieces of animal skins, pelts, teeth, wings, things that were there, and things I imagined. There were drums and rattles, stones too, something in the very centre, and long....

MARIA   I don't believe you're doing this! We went through all this at the rehearsals. We talked about why you weren't supposed to describe this, turn it into journalism. You told Hannah you wouldn't write it, you wouldn't talk about what happened in there. I believed you.

LINDA   I don't remember telling Hannah that.

MARIA   Linda, you can't talk about them, you can't expose them, you were invited into that circle to help you understand, not to write a book about it. No, there are no rules and regulations. Everytime someone says, 'Don't do something,' you always say, 'I thought you said there were no rules and regulations.'

There are no rules and regulations as such, but there is a

whole thing of respect, of sacredness. It's like that photograph of the man who snuck into the Sun Dance ceremony, you were offended by that photograph. Why? Because it did something to you when you were looking at it, it robbed you of something. Now you want to do the same thing, so some other little girl can come along and look at your words and feel the same way you did when you looked at that picture. Linda, it's your stuff now.

LINDA I wasn't offended by that picture, it inspired and touched me in a way I never forgot. Those guys that snuck in and painted pictures and tape-recorded and begged people to tell them things, were recording something that was dying, and I was able to see it, that picture made me want to learn more, know more, it was the beginning of teaching.

MARIA Listen to you, just listen to what you're saying – they 'snuck in' – but you were invited, asked to become a part of it, the doors were opened to you, we trusted you. And who told you it was dead or dying? Those men who snuck in? Do you want to learn by sneaking around? That attitude of 'dead or dying' is what's killing us.

LINDA Alright, I'll cut it all out.

MARIA No, not your experience. You're an artist, find a way to do it.

Enough to say that there were power objects in the ceremony ... and that somehow ... Maria was no longer beside me. My only security was taken away.

My fear had a new quality, different from the fear I usually lived with. It made sense. In this room, in this circumstance, it made total sense to be scared out of my mind. It seemed part of it, being alive in a scared kind of way. An electrical storm feeling.

I want to go farther so badly. Once I thought theatre and ceremony were the same, and still I feel their connection, but the sight ... there was theatre to this event, no question.

Hannah spoke, and I felt it was to me. 'There are people here who are not of this tradition, let them open their hearts to this ceremony, this healing, let them open their minds and hearts to what is to happen.'

Then there was darkness. Complete and utter blackness. Utter lack of light, sleeping bag, blanket tight, nailed shut against the farmhouse windows. There was only the moon and starlight to be shut out, but the feeling that light existed, anywhere in the world, was gone. I felt like I was exploding. I felt as if fear would burst through my skin if it could, so that my flesh would split open and the fear let loose in the room. The chanting rose up around me, something to concentrate on, something to follow with the senses. If I had been able to chant, if I hadn't been afraid of my uncertain voice mixed in with the strange nasal call of the people around me, then it might have been easier. But I felt myself to be still a watcher, as if the comforts of the cermony were not for me. The sounds pierced through securities, realities, and the sweet grass smell was like hands in my hair, fingers of smoke that changed the linear attack of my thoughts. My brain clung to the way it usually worked, but the smoke said, 'No, this channel also works.' Then Bear came in....

MARIA Don't do it.
LINDA I won't ... but how am I supposed to ...?

I wanted to feel like them so badly, believe like them, understand like them. My generalized mystical beliefs included all things, but I wasn't sure what to believe. Until I felt something in front of me.

The voice of the Bear was on the other side of the room, but something was in front of me. It was as tangible a feeling as if you have your eyes closed and someone's face is two inches from your face. There's a sense that tells you someone is very close, certainly that close. It was telling me something with a very practical certainty. No big deal, just that there was something very close to me. Then I got the feeling that the something was in a half circle around me. I felt like I was being touched very gently with an electric probe, my skin was tingling in response.

I felt the theatre of the ceremony, the 'performance elements,' as Paul would call them, but at the same time I felt something else, something called up by those elements, as if the theatricality was a signal, a lure. 'We imitate you, and through our imitation, you come.'

Meanwhile, on the other side of the room, someone was being named, and I heard people murmur in appreciation. Then Eagle came in, the chanting rose again....

MARIA Linda!
LINDA Just let me do this part.

MARIA You're acting like all those people who write culty little books:
'I went to Alberta and saw the light.' You're making this
whole thing sound so romantic, so mystical....

LINDA Okay, I'll stop. I won't write anything, we'll forget it. We
rehearsed a play, and we did it, period. But I say there's
something in this that's important, and you think so too, you
took me there. I've been up against the wall with this stuff for
seven years, and I'm still working at it. Give me that, I am a
romantic, that's the truth. When I see ... green arcs in the air....

MARIA And that's all they were – green lights. Don't make them into
anything else....

LINDA Just a romantic white girl in a corner, having her mind fried ...
okay?

MARIA You wanted your mind fried.

LINDA You're saying, 'You wanted something,' and I'm saying, 'Then
respect that I wanted something,' and you're saying, 'Then
respect the something you wanted.'

MARIA How about that, she finally heard me.

I don't remember how long Eagle stayed, but finally time caught
up, and somehow the ceremony was over. There was light. People
stirred and laughed, heading over to the trailer for the feast. Hannah and her helpers packed up. Maria came over to me. 'We'll sleep
here tonight.' 'Oh, no,' I thought, 'right here in the same room?' But
the spirits seemed to be gone. Later we took the sleeping bags from
the windows, rolled up in them on the floor, and went to sleep.

Rebellion

The next day we drove to Edmonton to begin rehearsals. I entered
them bolstered up by the energy of raw will.

The cast for this stage of the improvisational jam session was:
Graham Greene (not a relative of the famous author, but an Iroquois actor); Tantoo Cardinal, a mixed-blood actress who had been
involved in Native politics as well as theatre and film; Bob Bainborough, a white actor and one of the fellow creators of *Paper Wheat*,
who now performed with the Edmonton Second City Comedy
group; and me. Paul Thompson and Maria directed and fed in
energy and ideas.

I don't remember how we began. I remember the rehearsals in

fits and starts. I remember being more paranoid than I had ever been in my life. For sheer audacity this couldn't be beat. I stood up and acted out my impression of Maria Campbell to her face. I invented and acted out intimate scenes that had been confided to me in the privacy of the station wagon. I was beat up, shot up, starved, racially oppressed and spiritually robbed. I screamed obscenities at Graham Greene, who played Maria's lover. I made impossible comments about Native people, trying to imitate Maria's wry self-deprecation. She'd say, 'There go a bunch of Indians, all stuffed in a car, with two welfare checks between them.' I'd say, as Jessica, 'There the Indians go again, we shouldn't call it Native dancing, we should call it the welfare dance.' Nobody thought it was very funny.

MARIA Of course nobody thought it was funny, do you realize how appalled I was at myself when I heard you say those things? You were playing back my own self-hatred. I was making a joke about something that really hurt me and when Jessica said those things she was so flip, and I'd think, 'How could I say something like that?' And I'd think about how much I hated myself, and I'd get angry, and then would come the questions, the political analysis: 'How did that happen?' It was those white people that came along and did this to us, made us hate ourselves. Then I'd look up and there you'd be, one of them.

Stuffed with information, I felt like a prize goose. Everyone was hoping for a good pâté – just stuff a little more down the old trap and hope when we cut her open, there'll be something really tasty. I felt as if every day people gathered round to taste me, and went, 'Yuuuck.' But it wasn't my liver that was exploding, it was my head. And maybe my heart.

MARIA And we never talked.

LINDA Maybe if we talked, we would never have gotten through.

I was battering against a stubborn, rebellious, self-hating character, who was struggling with her own power. It was Maria, of course, or Jessica. It never occured to me, not for years, that it was me.

I had been told that this was not really a religion, but a spiritual path. I was throwing everything I could into the improvisations, but for days it seemed that every choice I made was wrong. 'You can't mention sweet grass in this way, you wouldn't talk about the spirits in that way.' From Maria's accounts of her own behavior with her teachers, she was highly rebellious. Her own quote from one of their fights was, 'You can take your spirits and stick them up your ass!' But when I played scenes with Tantoo, acting out those confrontations, I was told that Native people didn't talk to their elders like that. In what was a highly sexual piece, all of a sudden swearing was out, sexual references had to be guarded. Meanwhile Paul was coaching, 'More city edges, tougher, she's not from suburbia.'

I know now, there wasn't a sacred feather I didn't ruffle, a profound image I didn't tromp on, a gentle subtlety of culture I didn't scream out to the skies. All I felt were rules and more rules. I watched Maria turn into someone afraid of the very process she had begun. I wanted to shout, 'This isn't Native spirituality, this is the Presbyterian Church!'

MARIA Catholic Church. Linda, believe me. If you think you were uptight, I was devastated at myself. When I'd hear myself saying, 'No, no, no,' what I was hearing was a Catholic voice. When I had to confront this woman, who was all for revolution, all for change, who really believed in ... in the path she was following ... to listen to her, to look at her, she was the most conservative Catholic woman I had ever met in my life. Totally conservative. She was so uptight I couldn't imagine how she had ever done the things she had done. I could scorn Catholics, before I started to work on *Jessica*, because I thought I was free, I wasn't all bound up with that stuff. But I really was. For the first time in years and years, I found every time you said 'Fucking this and fucking that,' or you told Vitaline to shove things up her ass, I wanted to make the sign of the cross and moan the rosary. For the first time in my life, I had to deal with the woman I'd shoved away someplace. I almost went to church. I had to start looking at things in the Catholic faith, real things that came from the mother, from the grandmothers, and that looking helped me to understand for the first time why everybody's been Christian for so long. But it all confused me, shook up my easy theories, and I ended up with fears and uncertainties I thought I had already dealt with. I had to deal with 'her' and she wasn't easy.

The Native actors were inexperienced at improvisation, while the white actors had been making up material for years. They had to live with the frustration that their culture was being explored, and all too often maligned, without the technique to jump in and say their own piece. It was especially difficult for Tantoo, an actress on the verge of being able to tap an enormous talent. Here I was, leaping about, playing Maria, talking ignorantly about my life as a Halfbreed, about my spirits, and there was Tantoo, watching.

LINDA   I couldn't get your body. I couldn't get your voice. It was other things, like the age difference between us. I was trying to imagine you young. I was playing you ...

MARIA   ... younger.

LINDA   I mean, those flashbacks to Vancouver ... I couldn't imagine that person at all. So I was left on my own making up a character. You said the Metis are feisty. You said they loved life and weren't afraid of things and jumped in. So I jumped, but I didn't feel like you. Now I can see the girl whom you wrote about in *Halfbreed.* I couldn't see her then.

MARIA   I know you couldn't. And I didn't know how to make you, or help you see her.

LINDA   I had the picture. But the person speaking to me was so reserved. Quiet, dignified, removed ... I couldn't see the humour. I saw it, but it was as if we never really laughed....

MARIA   You mean you can see it now?

LINDA   Yes. Oh, yes.

MARIA   Strange ... but the stuff is there. All the words are there.

LINDA   But the person is me imagining myself as this ... Metis. Oh, God. Every time I'd go at all that Native stuff I'd be cringing inside. To have the 'subject' in the room, plus, they're Native and I'm as white as the driven snow, the clouds on the prairie, whatever. I mean, it's outrageous when I think about it. I can't believe we did it. I can't believe you sat through it. Scenes with nothing happening, but that's Thompson's process, Right? You don't stop a scene unless you're so far under, you're ready for the shovels. I believed that I could find it somehow. But I knew it was sounding awful. And the vibes! Oh, God. The energy from Tantoo, the vibes from ... you. I'm not saying that you were bad-vibing me – maybe I am saying that – but I understand now. I couldn't think what was going through your mind ... I couldn't! If I had, I wouldn't have been able to do it. So I had to be dumb.

Oh, I can see that room and I can see me getting up, full of bravado, and buzzing with the things you told me. I mean, I was in heaven. I'd been given the most wonderful stories, the most incredible character. I'd been to the ceremony. I had my head full of what had happened there. I was on fire with all this stuff. I'd go out and it would be ... shit! And I did it without knowing anything, Maria. I had read a few books. We'd traveled around for two weeks. I'd been to one ceremony. I didn't know anything.

I had no idea of the real powder keg that I was walking into. I knew I was getting a kind of racism, and I knew somehow I was putting out a kind of racism, but I didn't know what it was. Maybe my racism was in not accepting that there would be racism.

MARIA You couldn't see that person fighting back. You couldn't see that person shooting up. You couldn't see that person getting beat up, because I couldn't either. Somewhere along the way I'd removed myself from her.

LINDA Later, I saw her.

Whose Magic, Whose Oppression?

Maria tried to bring in the Celtic side of things, wanted me to explore what she saw as my own traditions, but I had no equivalent experience with that culture. I couldn't articulate that the work I was doing was already coming from a kind of 'Celtic side,' that the influence was within me – not as information to be tapped, but as a felt sense, fueling the improvisations she was watching. I could read as many books about Celtic goddesses as she wanted, but I was overwhelmed and fed by the Native world living and breathing in front of me. The first glimpse of the horror of their experience, and the wealth and wisdom of their culture, knocked me flat. But I had no time to be out cold on the floor, I had to come up with something. I called on the fighter part of me, it was the strongest thing I knew. My dukes went up, propelled by raw will. I would burst through, break through, think through, try through, but I would understand and deal with this problem.

MARIA While you were being overwhelmed with my history and my oppression, you were making me feel like it was exclusively mine. I couldn't understand why you didn't know your own history, never mind the magic and power stuff. My great grandfather was a Scot, hundreds of thousand of his people had starved in Scotland, Ireland and Wales, not even six hundred years ago. Their land had been taken away, given to the sheep. They starved to death, and when they left they died in masses on the ships coming over, many of them had been burned as witches, tortured. I couldn't understand why you didn't know that ... the history of your pain and all the things that happened to your people was exactly the same as our history. I couldn't understand why you refused to look at that. It seemed that that would be a meeting place for us.

You could say, 'This is what happened to my grandfathers,' and I could say, 'This is what happened to my grandfathers.' That's what made me angry, as if you wanted to believe that my people were the only ones that had suffered this, that my people had been the only ones that were conquered. At the same time, you and Paul would talk about universal themes, and I would get so angry. 'Universal,' I'd think, 'universal, what the fuck do you know about universal, when you think that we have an monopoly on oppression?' The books that I was suggesting you read talked about that oppression, the conquering of your people. I felt like what you guys were saying was that you wanted magic, you wanted power, but not history. But to me there was no separation, I didn't see how you could separate power, spirituality, sacred things, songs and stories from starvation, hunger, the taking away of land, because you can't. And again, we didn't talk.

LINDA For whatever reason, I could only absorb what was in the room, and what was in the room was you.

MARIA When I started to look into the Indian stuff, Indians never let me forget that I was part white so I'd look at this picture of my white grandfather, and there he was with this long white hair, big bushy beard, and these really fierce eyes. He looked like what I thought God looked like. In that picture he's sitting there with his knees spread out and his back like a poker, wearing moccasins and this funny little tam on his head. I didn't know what to do with him. So I started studying, reading all these books about the Scots and the Irish. I went to the societies and I found out that they had the same things, storytellers, music, sacred stones, mother earth, little people. They told me that when the British came they took the bagpipes away, banned them, because they knew that their music was sacred, gave them strength. They used to go into the caves with the 'chanters,' and teach the children how to blow on them so that someday, when they were able to have bagpipes again, the songs and the skill wouldn't be lost. The same conquerer who had taken my grandfather's land away, outlawed his culture, did the same to my grandmother here, on this land. Then I think, 'How could people who had been conquered in that way, come here and do exactly the same thing to Indians?' That's when I started to understand that when you're oppressed, it's easier to become the oppressor, you turn on your own. Just like walking into Indian Affairs and seeing guys there implementing things that will hurt their own people.

When I worked with you and Paul, I thought, here are university-educated people, they'll know all this stuff. This actress has a Welsh name, she must know all about the Welsh people. I figured you'd know more than me about your history, where you came from, and that we'd exchange. It took me ages to realize that you didn't know about that stuff, and then I was appalled. Passe Muraille was known to be a political theatre – how could you be political without knowing your own stories? And they were no different from the stories of Halfbreed or Indian people.

LINDA   Maria, you have no idea what it's like to have what happened to Native people, the whole of it, finally hit you. I had some sense of it – smallpox blankets, reservations, dispersals – but the more you showed me, the more I read, the reality of you and Tantoo and Graham in the room ... I didn't see 'the wrongs done Native people,' I saw that it had been genocide. Whatever weirdos are running around saying it didn't happen, the Holocaust is a reality to the Jews, to everyone, a part of history – six million people destroyed, the camps, Israel, all that.... But how can I describe to you what it's like to realize it happened here, and that no one remembered or

really knew, and now I was meeting the survivors? I was so
ashamed. There's no describing that shame, it just tore me
apart. Here was a religion, or a spiritual path, or whatever,
that I thought was so wonderful, and I knew that just twenty-
five years ago you could be jailed for drumming and burning
sweet grass – for praying? And there it was in the room. I felt
the pain and it overpowered me. The people I met, sure, I'd
seen rural poverty before, but here everybody was the same
colour. To visit reservations and see people sitting like that in
front of these falling down pay-off houses, to see their faces
and know my people had done this to them ... the shame of it,
the shock. Besides, I truly liked the people I met, and I think
they liked me. And now I knew what really had happened. If
you're Catholic and have any sense of guilt, justified or not, if
guilt can ever be right, or make sense, then I was drowning in
it. To stand in that rehearsal hall and have it all go 'ping,' this
is what happened ... it was overwhelming. Hard to stand up
and say, 'Oh, yeah, well, six hundred years ago in Scotland
my ancestors had a rough time too.'

MARIA   Paul did tell me that you couldn't control what happened in
this kind of rehearsal, that all you could do was put out the
information and see what the actors did with it.... It seemed
that where you wanted to go was into the spiritual stuff, the
spirits, and I couldn't understand, even if that was what was
going to happen, why you didn't bring in your own.

LINDA   I did, but mine turned out to be ... theatrical.

The Wolverine

As the jam continued, Maria and Paul would go away at lunchtime
and talk. I never knew what they said, I didn't want to know. I think
I didn't want to know. I would wait each day to hear the plan from
Paul. So far, there was no writing, only improvisation. I kept waiting for Maria to come in with some nice safe scenes for us all to play,
a rescue from the wide open terrors of improvisation, but she just
watched and vibed.

Paul introduced an exercise in which we became animal spirits. I
don't remember which one I picked, I only remember crawling
around on the floor, grateful that I didn't have to come up with my
awful imitation of Maria for a while. I was beginning to think she

had deliberately made herself inimitable. The actors related as animals, Bob Bainborough as Crow, Tantoo as Coyote, Graham as Bear, and me as who knows what. After rehearsals Maria and Paul began talking about the Wolverine. I was too soft, apparently. Maria fixed me with her green-eyed stare and delivered a spine-chilling description of wolverine habits and savagery. As she spoke, something came rushing in.

LINDA Your eyes were incredible, you started giving me all these images, just hitting me. And my stomach starts to churn and part of me thinks, ' No, I can't understand this, what am I going to do with it?' But another part was just dying to talk, dying to. I'd just broken up with someone I really loved and I felt somehow ... wrecked by being on tour so long by myself, wrecked by my whole theatre life ... and you just kept hitting me. I was just dying to be as ugly and as vicious and as black as I actually fucking felt inside.

After that, every day Paul would ask me to do the Wolverine, and every day I would say, 'Not yet.' It was rare for me to refuse to do anything. He would screw up his face and say, 'No?' And I would screw up my face and say, 'Not yet.' I could tell he thought I was chicken.

At night, I was experimenting with my own rituals. It felt good to be freed, to allow myself to meditate or pray or whatever it was, within the curtain of a project. It was as if I could say, 'I'm not really praying, I'm doing research.' I would set up a candle, a glass of wine, tobacco to be burnt, my eagle feather, a star-shaped piece of jewelry I had bought from Hannah, never one to ignore a good trade. Then I would try to re-experience the feeling of the ceremony, and the feelings of my childhood. I would reach out in my thoughts, then I would think of what I wanted to do the next day. It was only within these little rituals that I allowed myself to think about the wolverine.

Days passed, and once more I saw Paul coming toward me. He had this odd look on his face, like he'd given up, but once more he said, 'Are you ready to do the wolverine?' This time I said, 'Yes.' I could feel it coming, I was already half wolverine as I climbed the stairs to a stage area we rarely used. I wanted to be far away. Crouching down, arms outstretched, head up, I bared my teeth and hissed.

MARIA   I was watching, and I knew something was happening. But I
didn't know what it was, because lots of times you went up on
the stage like that and something happened. It's like knowing
when there's a Warrior walking in I could feel it coming with
you. When you went up there you knew what you were
doing, and when you started I saw the Wolverine, I saw his
teeth, his claws ... it wasn't you. I never saw you, and it was
freaky. I'd heard my dad talk about wolverines on traplines
and how trappers dread them. If they are caught in a trap and
haven't chewed their leg off before you arrive, they will fight
you to the death. If they manage to get away they won't leave
the area, they will stalk you, watching, waiting, then they'll
foul your trapline so that all other animals will move out;
they'll go into your cabin and do the same thing, as well as rip
and tear everything apart. They will, and can, ruin you. When
you looked out at us, that was the wolverine I saw. I was
freaked right out....

Sometimes when people say they are freaked out by me
and they think maybe I'm going to do something to them, I
know now that they must see that part of me. The part I never
see or want to, but I know is there, and when I looked at you,
there it was. You had changed. There was a ruff ... the
wolverine has a ruff that never frosts in the winter, a section
on his back that stands up like a Doberman when he's mad.
Wolverines almost have little hands, long-fingered, long-
clawed. They're very stocky, close to the earth. They're a
lump. And they have these incredible, delicate hands.... I'll
never forget the way you looked. I don't know what anybody
else saw. I only know what I saw ... and I remember watching
you and feeling my hands becoming claws too. You almost
pulled me in ... because when another wolverine comes ...
wolverines don't travel together ... only one wolverine owns
the territory. I wanted to go in there and just do it ... it was ... I
can't describe, Linda, what happened. I just knew that, no
matter what happened from then on, I couldn't take any more
chances. You know? Make sure you were protected. Make
sure I was protected. Make sure that we had a circle, because
who knows? Maybe you'd attack one of the other actors.
Because at that point, that Wolverine had no control. What
would have happened if it had pulled me in there? One of us
would have been alive when it was finished.

Never in my entire life has anything ever spooked me like that.

LINDA I remember that when I came out of it, I was standing. I looked to my side, and there was sunlight coming through the window. I felt released, light and free, I just felt cleansed. And I looked up and saw these white faces looking at me. You guys looked ... like, it was dead silence. And I thought that maybe this is the calm after a wonderful theatre performance and everyone's going to go, 'Wow. That was great.' But nobody said, 'Wow. That was great.' Nobody said anything. All that happened was this complete silence. Paul with that funny look on his face. I came down. He just sort of went, 'Well, ah ...' And then you came and you said, 'It's my fault.' All I could think was, 'What do you mean, what's her fault? What's anybody's fault? You said do the Wolverine. I've just done the Wolverine. What's the problem here?' You said, 'It's my fault we didn't do the circle at the beginning and at the end of rehearsals.' And I was really mad. 'Why are you all so freaked out? This is the whole purpose of the rehearsal.' It didn't mean I wasn't glad in some way. When we actually sat down and did that circle, I was glad, but I felt chastised. It was like I was having my knuckles wrapped because I'd done something bad, and yet I knew it was good. So how could good be bad? The whole time in rehearsals I had this feeling that what was good was bad and what was bad was good. When I was good, it was bad, because I was transgressing into this other territory. When I was bad and safe, then I was good, because I wasn't transgressing. One of the things that started making me crazy was I couldn't tell any more.

Paul called an early lunch, unusual for him because he doesn't like to break concentration with mundane things like food. The actress in me was furious and betrayed. I knew I had reached beyond my experience and spoken true words. I didn't expect compliments, but I didn't expect to be treated like a leper. By the standards of the theatre gods, I had done 'good work'. But where were the theatre gods now?

MARIA I thought I had taken you totally into a dark side and couldn't do anything to protect you. I should have been doing our circle every morning and every night, but of course I hadn't.

For years I had done that, did it only when I thought I needed it, I don't know why, just to be rebellious or something....

So when something came into my life that scared me, or was totally out of my control, then I'd remember and do it, like the child that's been told over and over again, 'There are things that can happen to you on this road so you must protect yourself every day. Do your circle in the morning and at night, then you'll be okay.' That's the warrior's way. Well, I'm a very lazy warrior.

We needed what Maria called, 'protection.' It was a word I heard a great deal later on. To me, all rehearsals were protected by their very nature, especially improvisational rehearsals in which everything had to come from a kind of immediate, wide-open frequency. Theatre was already blessed, it didn't need more blessings to protect it from being theatre. Maria explained that we should have been forming a circle at the beginning and end of each rehearsal, as if the rehearsal was a ceremony. To her, I had played with fire. How could I say that 'playing' was my ritual? It took Maria a long time to hear the theatre gods.

MARIA What theatre gods? Nobody ever told me about theatre gods. All I knew was that I hadn't done what I was supposed to do, all I knew was the Creator, the grandmothers, grandfathers, and the rituals that they required. When you said, 'We're protected,' I didn't know what the hell you were talking about. Nobody explained anything, explaining wasn't part of Paul's process.

The only tape recording that is missing from the original session in Edmonton is the tape of the Wolverine. I heard it once, two years later, and understood the look on people's faces that day. My voice was chilling, unrecognizable. Then the tape disappeared.

The Trade

Meanwhile, characters were being formed. Tantoo worked on a character based on her grandmother. It was through this old lady of Tantoo's that I began to understand Native humour. It was so wry, it had an underground sense too, as if white people maybe be listening so certain things couldn't be said.

Bob Bainborough became Crow. He was laconic and tough. He did nothing imitative or crow-like at all, but when you looked at his face, the eyes seemed beady and dark, the nose became a focal point as if all his energy was concentrated there, his knees became pointed, and the whole body tilted backwards, as if surprised at human behavior. Bob also developed the role of the lawyer, later named after him.

Graham Greene played Bear and Jessica's lover, Sam. He became Bear so naturally, seemed to swell in size and weight. As Sam, he spent a long time pretending to beat me up, and sometimes the scenes were frightening and off centre in a way I had never experienced before. Again, we were acting out to Maria some of the most horrendous moments of her life. And doing it badly. Yet Graham had enormous strength and tenderness that later became part of Sam.

Paul and Maria constantly bopped us back and forth between the personal, spiritual and political angles of the puzzle. One day, after talking with Maria at lunch, Paul had another one of his impossible ideas. He went on about the Irish and Native peoples having developed a similar love of pain. He talked about the great dirges and songs of Ireland, the idea that a conquered people make language and art out of how bad things are. As he was speaking, I began to hear a kind of beat. I crawled to the middle of the space on my hands and knees, and started pounding out a rhythm on the floor. I saw flashes of dark drunk faces, saw ale in jugs. They could have been mixed-bloods of the New World, or dispossessed Scots, Irish, and Welsh of the Old.

'We're drinking tonight, for a change, for a change, we're drinking tonight for a change. We're drinking the tears of a thousand years, we're drinking tonight for a change.' I went on for five transcribed pages. I pounded out the story of the second Riel Rebellion, not the Highland Clearances. At the end I was panting, my eyes searching the others for just a little sense of yea or nay. But there was nothing but Paul's face, herding us all into another scene. I felt like the workhorse.

The session was three weeks long. At the end we talked briefly about what had happened, unable to go on about how wonderful it had been. Paul said that we had definitely tapped some power, and that was all we could say. Maria seemed happy it was over. I didn't know how I felt. Somehow we had to come up with a play for the fall and I didn't know what was planned. Were we all going to try this again, and work the play as a collective creation? Oh no.

MARIA After the rehearsal in Edmonton, Paul and I drove back to Regina. I tried to convince him to use another actress, instead of you. I told him I wouldn't work with you again. I almost did it, I almost had him convinced, but he said if that happened then he would have to go, and, well, he couldn't go, if he did I wouldn't learn the process. In the end we made a trade, and you stayed.

LINDA Don't tell me what the trade was, I don't want to know.

The God of the Fiddle Players

Back in Toronto, Paul revealed the plan. I would improvise the entire play myself. Paul always had great ideas like that; at first inspiring, until you realize you're out there on a cliff somewhere performing to the seagulls. Paul would direct and help with structure, Maria would be there with stories and everything else. The three of us would work alone.

In a way, I was relieved. I thought I'd be freer with just Maria and Paul in the room. For the last few years I had already stepped outside of my role as a group improvisor and it was hard to go back. I wanted to be the dreamer. Within the realm of collective creation, that's a no-no. Everybody's the dreamer. That's why there isn't a 'writer.' It's very rare that the contemplative ego of a writer and the active sibyls of improvisation can work together. In this case, I was being asked to be both. And in the middle of all this redefinition were our thin-skinned creative egos....

We worked in the tiny Backspace of Theatre Passe Muraille, a narrow black tunneled box that gives the impression of being underground. There seemed less fear in the room this time. We shut out the brilliant late summer sun and began to cook.

LINDA Before you came I did one session alone with Paul. He said, 'Just be her. Stop talking.' Because I would start motor-mouthing, hoping that words would bring something, so at least there'd be writing done if there wasn't a true character. But this time I just sat in a chair for about an hour, and every time I would try and do something, he would stop me and I'd go back to the chair. I just sat there, as you. That was the entry to what we did in Toronto.

The first day, buoyed up by Maria and Paul, grounded by the work already done by Tantoo, Bob and Graham, I could see the beginnings of a through line. I knew how Jessica arrived at the beginning of the play, bruised, paranoid and crazy with the voices in her head. She had gone too far with the Wolverine and didn't know how to come back. Then I became Vitaline, an old spiritual teacher, keying into Tantoo's old lady character, drawing on Maria's frustrations with Hannah. Vitaline created a new ceremony, incorporating the dress-up of the street world, and the machines of the city. I could hear Maria's laughter. The characters bopped back and forth, creating scenes, talking to each other. It was as if some line had been relaxed. I was no longer afraid of crossing the border from sacred to theatre, because Maria seemed no longer afraid.

MARIA There was this part of me that said, 'You don't know what the theatre is.' And I guess I still don't know what the theatre is. I don't know if it's sacred or not.

LINDA No one knows what the theatre is, and no one knows if it's sacred or not. The god of the theatre is sort of Dionysus, right? And no one is ever sure about him. No one is ever sure if that guy just wanted to drink wine and screw all the girls, or whether he was.... It's like Pan, there's not a clear reading on that guy and everyone in the theatre knows it.

MARIA I started doing my research about who the patron of the theatre was. There's no god of the theatre, for Christ's sake. At least not an official one that I could find. But I felt much more comfortable and started to relax when I realized ... that it was sort of like the fiddler for me, the god of the fiddle players. Because no matter what happens, no matter how drunk he gets, no matter how lecherous he gets, he comes from a spiritual place.

LINDA But dangerous.

MARIA But dangerous.

By this time, tension was building in the white theatrical community that was aware of the struggle for Native rights in the arts. Tension was also building in the Native community, at a time when professional Native theatre was just beginning, but there were times when the white liberals were the most vehement. To the outside world there was a play called *Jessica*, with a lead part that was going to a white actress. It was impossible to explain that there was no play yet, no part called 'Jessica' to be handed out to anyone. As rumours spread through the microcosm of the theatre, *Jessica* was being born. No matter how many phone calls and emotional explosions occurred, Maria stood firm. No one was going to tell her who she should work with, no one was going to tell her how to learn about theatre.

In the middle of all the controversy about the show, we went to a club called the Horseshoe Tavern. A Native woman recognized Maria. She said, 'I hear you've been having some trouble with that play. I've got a gift for you, for the play, someone should wear it.' She dug into her handbag and pulled out an old brown paper bag. Maria opened it, and inside was an obviously precious object. Hanging from thick blue and white beads, strung on rawhide, was a bear claw. It looked ancient. In the performances in Saskatoon, Graham, as Bear, wore the necklace, ripping off his shirt at one point to expose it. He never failed to get a gasp from the Native people in the audience. The white people didn't really get it. Through another strange twist, that same necklace is now in the hands of Al Pacino. The spirit's weird humour again.

The gift cleared the air once more.

Brown Like Me

Maria was experimenting with the makeup I would wear in the show. It was advisable to, as Paul put it, 'brown up'. Maria decided we should put me to the test. There was a graduation of high school students at the Native Friendship Centre and she took me there as her guest. Before we left, we worked on my makeup. It was strange, but when I looked at my face, there did seem to be a change. Was this 'Brown like Me'? But I felt relaxed around Native people in a way I'd never felt before. It was like wearing an invisible cloak. I walked down the halls of the centre feeling like a Native woman, treated as a Native woman. There was a short ceremony at the beginning of the dinner. Maria whispered instructions to me but, as she said later, I could easily have been a Halfbreed who had been brought up white. At one point a white man came into the room. I couldn't believe what I felt. Everyone pulled in, as if to protect themselves. I pulled in too, in a moment of complete identification. Maria leaned over and said, 'Now you know what it's like. If you'd come into the room as a white person, that's what would have happened.' We went to the washroom at some point, and she got out her makeup and did a touch-up quite openly, without the least sense of embarrassment. We were laughing like schoolgirls, as she blended in the streaks on my face.

The Song

All this time I was waiting for the courage to do the rape scene. One day, in the darkness of the Backspace, I was Jessica, twelve years old, and two men came to the door, looking for my father. I felt angry and scared, talking with my head down to these big white people. I knew they had the power to put us all in jail if they wanted. I saw them stomp around the house, checking in corners for poached game, I saw them look at me. 'Are you alone here?' I didn't answer. Then I was down on the ground, they were prying my knees apart, I was screaming and biting, and they were holding me down. I felt something go up deep inside me, opening me up like a can of food. I lay spread-eagled on the ground for a long time, hanging onto the floor and sobbing. Then I curled into a ball, and from a cracked voice, came a lullaby: 'Tour a lour a laura....'

When I looked out into the room, Maria was gone. I found her standing behind the risers, tears rolling down her face. I was afraid to face her.

LINDA I knew that was stuff you didn't want to give, but you gave it to me. I felt like I knew what happened, I don't know if I saw the actual room, I saw a room ... I don't know if I sang the song you maybe sang, or if you sang anything, but....
MARIA You really did sing the song.
LINDA My mother sang that song.
MARIA My mother too....

For once I was able to act instinctively around her, I just opened my arms. As we held each other, it was as if I'd unleashed my own memories. Not a story, or even acting, but something else.

This Goddess Stuff

I was still hammering away at any mysteries I could get my hands on. I came in with a garbage bag full of brightly coloured scarves. I wanted to tackle this goddess stuff and I had some kind of an idea.

I poured the scarves out and tied myself up in them, not an easy thing to do. Finally I was blindfolded, feet tied, hands behind my back. I knelt and began an invocation to every goddess I could remember, hoping one of them would answer. All the ancient names that had only been printed words poured out of me, making a kind of chant. I struggled with my bindings, as I had been struggling with this 'her,' finally releasing myself in a bizarre kind of dance.

When I looked up, I heard the sound of clapping. It was Maria, looking mischievous. Paul looked confused, I could hear him thinking, 'How are we going to fit this in?'

MARIA That scene was incredible. After the rape it was the most
natural thing to do. I couldn't understand why Paul couldn't
see that. As I watched you break free of the bindings and
dance, my instinct said, for the second time, 'Yes, she hears the
same music that I do.' The rape broke something inside, the
dance healed, erased all the previous hurts of the rehearsal.
After that, we started fresh again.

White Speed

Each night, Maria and Paul transcribed the tapes so we had a record of what had been done. As I dashed my way through, playing Sam, Liz, Jessica, Vitaline, Bob, Wolverine, Bear, and miscellaneous characters throughout, we had time to do each idea only once. When I asked Paul when we were going to put it all together and work on it, he said, 'There's no time, we've got it written down, we'll give them this.' He was pointing to the raw transcriptions of the improvs. I couldn't believe it. I wanted to run at those transcriptions, stay up all night, make them good, edit, hone, work away. But I knew he was right, I knew that I didn't know how to make it better. None of us did. We had to wait for 'the grandmothers.' Every time Maria said that, I got the old white speedy feeling in the pit of my stomach. The grandmothers seemed to enjoy waiting until the last minute to come through.

At the end of the three weeks in Toronto, we had a pile of paper, an order of some kind for the scenes, and an opening night very soon.

Dangerous Territory

Whatever tenuous security I had found in Toronto soon vanished when we hit the west again. In Saskatoon Maria seemed to change. We were back in dangerous territory again, in the middle of her community and home. She was my Geiger counter; if she doubted me, or was afraid, I lost what little grounding I had found.

When the actors first read the roughly assembled play out loud, I felt I couldn't let go of the words. I had played all these scenes. Tom Hauff, who replaced Bob Bainborough as Crow and the lawyer, said, 'You're going to have to let go of it now, and just play your own part.' I felt like hitting him. Which was my part?

The rough script was constantly being edited and changed as we went, so there was still a certain amount of improvising going on. Whole paragraphs would be changed without a word to me. I was told, 'A Native person wouldn't say that.' I was supposed to be without ego, a vessel, claiming nothing. The more I tried to be the self-effacing vessel of the piece, the more owly I became. The real gift, as Paul so often reminded me, was Maria's. She had handed me her life, her philosophy and entry to her deepest self. When I complained to him about the restrictions and nudges of racism I felt from her, Paul would say, 'She lives here, you'll go back to Toronto, to a totally different life, and she'll take the repercussions of what we do. You have to understand the enormity of her risk.' I could only agree with him, yet I knew I also was risking something. The dividing line had been lost.

MARIA   It was just before the play opened, and I was starting to get totally freaked out. You would have this ... your eyes were ... you had this big round look, you looked like....

LINDA   Oh, don't make that face!

MARIA   Your eyebrows were raised right up, like someone was pulling you up from your hair, and you were staring at me. Your eyes were all pale. You looked as though, if I just touched you, you'd have shattered like a fine piece of glass. But at the same time you were asking me to fill that glass with wine. I'd never seen anybody like that. I got angry at Paul, 'What's he doing to her?' I mean, we were all doing it, but he was supposed to know what he was doing. If I let out what I was feeling to you, it would have been like hitting you, shattering you, and I knew I wouldn't be able to put you back together, because you were so greedy.

LINDA That's where I would say there was a possibility I was in real danger, because I had no sense of self protection....

MARIA You were in danger. I knew you were. I absolutely totally knew you were in danger. If anything would have happened to you, I would have laid my life on the line for you. That may be why I couldn't talk. Something inside me said, 'Don't do it.'

LINDA I'd see your eyes and think, 'I've done something wrong. What have I done wrong?' I was getting mixed signals – total encouragement and total resentment at the same time. I'm not saying the work was always great ... oh no no....

MARIA But definitely the power was there. And what freaked me was that my head told me you hadn't been there before, so I'd give you wsssshhhhhhhh ... all this stuff that everybody felt was negative energy, but it wasn't. I had to give you something to ground yourself with; that was supposed to be my job, to protect you when you went over to those places and you might fall off. But I wasn't happy about what was happening, I wasn't happy.

LINDA Yeah.

MARIA I mean, a part of me was overjoyed. That's why I was able to put out so much. But another part thought, 'Holy shit. What's going to happen to her if I can't help her, and what's going to happen to the community when they see this and think I've been telling her things?' And then I'd tell myself, 'No, she's strong, she'll be okay, and I haven't been telling her stuff, I only told her what I wanted her to know, so why is this other stuff coming out?' And then I'd look at Paul, waiting for him to say, 'It's okay, I know what's happening.' But he'd look at me like he didn't know what was happening.

The elders of the community were our ultimate judges. From one point of view, Maria was doing something blasphemous, she was going to put things on stage that many of her people believed should never be performed, by whites or Natives. Like a riddle – 'When is a ceremony not a ceremony? When is religion religion and when is it theatre?' We didn't have an answer and neither did Maria. She had stuck by me so often, but I wondered if the pressure would make her crack.

MARIA   I'd come away from the rehearsals wasted, and go to Paul
angry. I became even more fearful, not only for you, but also
for myself, because if something happened I wouldn't have
anything left in me to give. That, coupled with the fear of my
community not understanding what I was doing and
denouncing the play.... The community became a kind of
enemy to me, but that's not what was happening at all. I'd go
home after rehearsals, wasted, and just lock myself in my
room. I'd come out, and there would be three or four Native
women, making pots of tea, cleaning up, cooking for me. They
gave me back some of what I was putting out, they were the
community, but my fear blinded me to that.

In rehearsals, once more, I felt judgement. 'She can't do it, she can't
understand us, it's impossible.' I became jealous of Maria and Tantoo, of their blood relationship that reached back so far, so deep.
They laughed together in corners and I felt it was at me. In *Halfbreed*
Maria describes going into town as a child with her Metis clan,
watching the adults walk automatically with their heads down,
ashamed around whites who so clearly thought them inferior.
Now I walked with my head down around Native people. I felt
ashamed, I felt them watching my skin.

Things finally blew up. Maria and Paul had invited a woman
from a small Native newspaper to come in and watch rehearsals. I
didn't want a strange Indian woman to watch me struggle with
being Native. It was too much. But I was afraid to protest. It was
against Paul's process to be insular and private, at any time, in any
way. If you worked with him, you had better pretend to be free and
open. Besides, with all the racial tension in the air, I was afraid it
would appear racist if I said what I felt. The woman came, and I
went into my shell. When she left, I finally complained, and Maria
stormed out of the rehearsal hall.

MARIA   That was when I tried to hit you with my cowboy boot. I'd
quit drinking coffee, I'd quit smoking because you were
having trouble with your voice, I'd been smoking herbal
cigarettes and finally chucked them out, and I'd gone five
days without anything at all ... and then you acted like such
an asshole ... I remember we were taking a break, and I bent
down to put on my boots and you came over, knelt beside me
with that look on your face, and said 'I'm sorry, Maria.' I had
my boot in my hand and I just hauled off to whack you one, I

think it was Paul that pulled me off, maybe it was Tantoo. I
got to the street, I was so mad, and Tantoo grabbed me, sat me
down in a coffee shop, didn't say a word. Then she planked a
cup of coffee down in front of me and said, 'Drink it.' She then
lit a cigarette, put it in my mouth, and just centred me. I
thought, 'That's it, she's on her own now, I'm not giving her
anything anymore.' We went back to rehearsals, and I was
just blank to you. I blocked you. I left without saying
anything.

When I think of Paul, six years later, humour returns, but it's taken
that long. Here he was, strung between the egos of two emotional
and demanding women, each one holding a different key to the
play we were trying to make. He'd run one way, then the next,
explaining me to Maria, and Maria to me. Later he said it was his
turn to become a woman.

I went back to the place we were staying that night, feeling crazy.
Since the script had only been spoken once, I still needed to learn
my lines, but for some reason they wouldn't stay in my head. I had
taken to working with a bottle of brandy beside me. I'd learn a few
lines, and have a swig, learn a few more lines and have another
swig.... Often I learned the speeches and scenes in tears, dreading
the next day. But this night was the worst. I had offended Maria,
and if Maria deserted me, I was dead.

The next morning I went to rehearsals, once more terrified to
look her in the eye. But she said, 'I want us to form the circle again.
It's my fault that we've stopped doing it every day.' So we all sat on
the floor, and she addressed the grandmothers and grandfathers,
burned sage and began to speak. We didn't get very far before I was
sobbing so hard there was a pool of snot on the floor in front of me.
That's what I remember, the snot pouring down like the mucus of a
newborn. I'm not exactly sure what Maria said, but it was a beauti-
fully spoken apology. She admitted that she and Tantoo had begun
to close me out, and acknowledged the difficulties of the whole sit-
uation. I sat with my head bent down.

MARIA There were times when I asked you if you wanted to go
someplace, do something. No, you had to go and do some
work. You wanted to be alone. And so I respected that space.
But I had screaming matches with Paul when we'd leave
those rehearsals sometimes.

LINDA I wonder what he thinks.

MARIA He'd just say ... that's the process.

LINDA Yeah.

MARIA I'd say to Paul, 'It's going to happen now, she's going to break now,' and you'd come in and be ... giggling in this really strange way. I'd say, 'Hi. How are you?' And you'd go, 'Everything's fine. I'm fine. I'm cold.' Giggling away. And I knew you weren't fine and you weren't cold. Even to this day, when you start getting like that, I know....

LINDA She's gonna crack.

MARIA That's not cracking. That's the warning bell.

LINDA But I think what Paul was hanging onto ... was knowing that I wanted ... that my hunger ...

MARIA Oh, I know.

LINDA ... was strong enough....

MARIA And he convinced me of that....

LINDA Yeah.

Power Song

At the end of the play, Jessica had to discover and sing her power song. Maria asked Tantoo to take me down to the river and teach me how to chant. On a crystal-cold Saskatoon night, Tantoo and I walked down to the banks of the South Saskatchewan River. The snow had a hard crust and we walked high above the ground until we found a spot. Tantoo explained that you can chant anything, and asked me what songs I knew. We tried a Hank Williams tune, then some Beatles, then just free-form chanting, right out to the river and up to the stars. There was no time to be shy, I just wailed any way I could. She would chant, I would answer, following her with my wobbly voice. She never made me feel stupid, no matter what kind of sounds came out. Still, I had an image of myself on stage in brown greasepaint and borrowed feathers, singing a power song, with the elders going, 'You've got to be kidding.' I deked around that song for weeks, never really finding it in rehearsal, but knowing somewhere that it would happen, 'on the night,' or not at all.

Somehow, we were opening. Women appeared from nowhere and cooked a Metis feast, with bannock, chokecherry jam and buffalo stew. The elders would be there, the Native political community would be there, the white theatre audience and critics would be there. We formed the circle before we went on, smudging ourselves in smoke to feel cleansed and protected.

Maria had worked out an explanation for the play, so that the actors asked for a blessing, and were protected by that blessing. The idea was that repetition of the invocation accumulated power and strength each time it was spoken. All of the actors that play Jessica now, call on the strength of the previous Jessicas, so that they, in a way, become the grandmothers of the play itself. Jessica began:

N'Okoomuk, N'Mooshoomuk
(grandmothers, grandfathers)
Aye sake seean Ooma oota Ka nee poweeyan
(I am afraid as I stand here)
Aye koh tse Ka quay tsim tah kok Ka wee chi hee ache
(So I ask you for your help)
Quay chim tin now wow Muskow tay hay win Ka me ee ache
(I ask you to help me to have a strong heart, to have strength)
Quask Kah At chimoo yan
(To tell this story honestly and with dignity)
Ikquasi Hiyee Hi
(I've finished my circle, I give thanks)

The grandmothers were with us. The show was ragged, but powerful. The song happened. The audience stood at the end. I wanted to feel good, but something was dead inside, a piece of black coal in the middle of me that wouldn't go away. I knew I had done the best I could, but underneath I sensed there was trouble brewing. Paul dashed backstage, ecstatic with the response. Then Maria came back, looking shaken. We formed the circle at the end of the show, and it seemed to calm her down.

When the reviews came out I was criticized, not for my performance, but for my position, racially, in the play. It was, again, the white liberals who took exception. The Native community was practical enough to realize that a venture of this size usually had some white people in it. The elders were happy, seeing that the line between performance and religion had been carefully trod. Tantoo glowed, playing a double role that was made for flying. The major review wondered why she was not playing Jessica. That hurt, there was no way to explain. Again and again, Maria would reassure me that Jessica was not an 'Indian part,' that she was a mixed-blood woman, and either side of her could be brought out by an actress willing to truly take on the role. But I had lost the capacity to listen.

Squaw

One night after the show, Tantoo, Maria, and I were walking down
Twentieth Street on our way home. A bunch of guys drove by in a
pickup truck and yelled at us. I asked Maria what they were yelling.
'Squaws,' she said, then laughed, 'Now you've had just about
everything happen, you've even been called a squaw.'

As the run went on, I became more and more confused. We
began drinking and partying a lot as a cast. I never knew until later
that Maria disapproved of our behavior, I only knew that she
became more and more distant. One night before the show I sat
down to 'brown up,' and the makeup refused to stick to my skin. I
had always felt weird about putting it on, especially with Tantoo
behind me, who clearly didn't need makeup to play her part. My
sense of guilt over playing Jessica had become an obsession. I
started to panic as, again and again, I smeared on the colour, and it
beaded up and streaked as if repelled by the chemicals of my skin.
My hands started to shake, I broke out in a sweat, and we had to
hold the curtain. Maria was in the house, and she came down to
help me. After she calmed me down, we got the makeup to even out
a bit, but even then there were streaks at the side of my face that just
wouldn't blend in. Naturally, I took it as a sign.

The Break

Eventually some kind of contract between us had to be worked out.
I had no experience with working out contracts, and no energy to
really care. I usually just went along with whatever was suggested,
that whole area had always been Paul's territory. He asked me if I
wanted anything to be put in writing. Out of my paranoia and confusion came a little voice: 'Yes,' I said, 'I wouldn't mind having a
first refusal on the part of Jessica if it's ever done again.' I knew the
role had to be given to a Native woman the next time it was produced, maybe forever after. Yet I was seared by it, both a creation of
it, and it's creator. Strange as I felt playing the part, the thought of
never playing her again was unthinkable. It was as if my blood was
within it. I was afraid I would be left an outsider, officially 'one-
third' writer on a project I might never be able to touch again, either
as writer or actress. The chance to play Jessica again seemed a small
thing to ask.

In a dark lounge at the Bessborough Hotel, Paul handed over the pages of the contract he had put together with 25th Street House Theatre. I barely looked at it. By that time I could barely focus enough to read. I never heard any more about the contact until the day we left Saskatoon.

I looked for Maria on the final night, but she wasn't there. I knew something was wrong. The next day I phoned her. I was again the brittle, cheerful cheerleader, thanking her politely for everything she had done, asking about the future of the project. She said, 'I never want to have anything to do with you or Paul again. As far as I'm concerned, you can take the play and do whatever you want with it.' She said she had consulted a lawyer, that she wasn't signing anything. She said Paul and I had gone behind her back and she wasn't having any of it. I begged her to talk, discuss it, explained that the contract was just a starting place, no one expected her to sign if she had serious problems with it, but she wouldn't listen and hung up. I stood with the telephone in my hand for a long time. The contract was a red herring. It had just been too much and the energy had exploded. What we had tried to do was impossible. I flew home, my insides shredded, feeling like I could hear what people were thinking.

MARIA   When the production was finished in Saskatoon, I still didn't know what 'the process' was. I didn't know what the fuck had hit me. All I knew was that there was this play and everybody was excited. The play was good, but I couldn't understand why I went around feeling like I wasn't inside of me anymore. Paul never told me the process meant that.

LINDA   I don't think he knew.

MARIA   When I think of it today, the anger I felt had little to do with the contract. I mean, all the contract did was reinforce what I was believing. I felt betrayed, and thought, 'It's my fault. I was the one that believed Paul was my friend, and trusted him.' The anger was at myself. I was empty. But when I look at it now, what absolutely devastated me was that I had been looking after you, because I believed he was going to look after me. That didn't happen ... I didn't know what the hell had happened ... you'd done it before ... but I felt like here was everybody leaving....

Honest to God, Linda, I didn't have a clue who the fuck I

was. I didn't know anything. I felt like I was in a tunnel and it was about 150,000 miles long, and there was a light at the other end, and I had been at that light when I started out. Now the play was over, and I stepped back, outside of the theatre world, and I didn't have anything, and here's everybody packing up and leaving, and all of a sudden I'm at the other end of this tunnel, it's black and long and I don't even know where my stuff is. I don't know who I am. I don't know where I am. I don't know anything. But I know at the end of the tunnel is a light, and I have to get there if I'm going to survive. I thought, 'The play's over now and we can stop worrying about the actors, I can sit down with Paul and he will explain to me what the process was and I will understand it. Somehow I believed that understanding the process would help me find myself. But he didn't. He was just blank. There was this man I didn't know looking at me. With the contract. It just added to the fear, the sense of loss. It was horrible ... it was a horrible time. I was so angry, I didn't want to strangle you, I wanted to fucking claw everything to death. Just rip you apart.

I went out to the land, walked and raged around out there. It was winter. I didn't have any money. I was flat-ass broke. I was living off the money my daughter Roxanne had, about three hundred dollars a month ... I couldn't work ... I was sick. Not sick at what happened, but sick inside. I walked and walked and walked. Like in *Jessica*. Everything was barren, dead. There weren't any leaves. There weren't any flowers. There was just fucking nothing. I'd walk into the house and think, 'I've got to get myself together. Somehow I've got to find a way.'

I'd walk up and down that river road and think of all the things I could do to both of you. I thought I could take you to court, have a press conference, get a lawyer.... I'd walk through each scene and I'd think of what would happen to you guys when it was finished.

Then one day, something ... happened to me ... because, you see, that was the other thing, I'd stopped having dreams, I'd stopped hearing anything. It was like all the spirits had left me all by myself. They'd left with you. They were Wolverine and Crow and Bear and Coyote, and they were all

gone, the grandmothers were gone. I didn't have anyone to
call. I tried everything, and nothing came. I couldn't pray.
Then, that one day ... I'd walked so much and raged so much
and talked out loud so much, I finally just cried.... Then the
voices came back, I could hear them. They said, 'It's okay. You
did what you were supposed to do and we'll look after you.'

'But what was I supposed to learn in this process?' I
asked.... There wasn't any reply, just an image. A circle of old
women who didn't look at me, didn't say anything, just the
circle. But I was okay. I wasn't over the anger, but I felt like I'd
grounded a bit. I left it at that, and everything sort of picked
up. I was able to centre myself and figure out what I was
going to do next. A few weeks later I had a job, and much later
I went to Banff.

That Feeling

There was no contact between Maria and I for two-and-a-half
years. I tried to forget *Jessica*. Once or twice Paul suggested working
on it again, as if it was just any play, just any project, as if we could
just pick up the phone and call Maria. I'd look at him as if he was
crazy. Yet every time he mentioned it, he echoed something deep
inside me, that feeling in the pit of my stomach.

I co-wrote another play, *O.D. on Paradise*, I acted in movies and
television, and I blocked out a great deal of what happened. It was a
clear case of Pandora and the bundle that shouldn't have been
opened. I didn't want to see those dark weird beasties again. Some
things stayed – my education stayed, I burned sweet grass, I prayed
every once in a while, I thought of the earth as a being and not a
thing. 'He' was no longer a reasonable way to describe a creative
power. When I saw Native people on the streets, I felt kinship. As
for the play, I didn't see how it could ever be done. I stuffed all the
papers from the show into a crate beside my bed. The crumpled
edges of the script stuck out, getting covered with coffee and ashes.

The Rewrite

I was in New York, acting at the Public Theatre, when things finally
broke. I thought I was gone – I was moving to the States to finally
enter a world of true careerism in the grand old style. But there was

always *Jessica* over my head. The play I was doing, *Fen*, by Caryl Churchill, had a kind of mystical scene at the end, and every night I would listen to the audience. And every night I would feel drawn back to all that potential sitting in a bloody crate in my room.

Meanwhile, on the home front, our play *O.D. on Paradise* was libelled by a major newspaper, and as a result the police were called in to Theatre Passe Muraille, my personal life was in a shambles and, of course, there was *Jessica*. I would try desperately to keep up with the 'gotta own this town' furies, all the while thinking about Passe Muraille and wolverines and Metis fiddlers, all the while drinking tequila cocktails with New York actresses, trying to find the best agent. I remembered walking along the river at The Crossing, during one of the worst times in rehearsal. I had made a promise to the grandmothers then, that I would continue working until *Jessica* was complete, no matter what happened.

Finally, my whole body seized up and I returned to Toronto, bedridden for months. As I lay in bed, I still wouldn't touch that crate. But I could always talk. I began to tell stories to my visiting friends, stories about the rehearsals with Maria and Paul, the ceremony, the traveling, even about the wolverine.

LINDA I didn't know what to do. I knew I needed time to just lie there and think about it, and I thought about it for two months, lying in that bed. That was when Clarke Rogers became artistic director of Passe Muraille. He knew I was thinking about *Jessica* and I just said, 'I don't want you to tell anyone.' I knew I should talk to Thompson, but I didn't want to deal with anyone that was part of that whole mess. I did not understand it. I didn't understand what we are talking about now. I just felt this need ... and the misunderstanding with you! I had no idea where that was coming from.

So, finally, I started ... very carefully ... to make notes, read all those books again, listen to the tapes. And then I would stop myself: 'You can't do this ... da da da.' Then the thoughts would start coming back.... I was crying half the day. I was a complete bloody mess, phoning up my friends, just in tears and tears and tears and tears, not knowing what the hell was happening to my body ... the pain alone.... Everybody moved out of the house. That's my novel: an actress lying in bed, in a house with four people, three of them move out, leaving her there, taking all the furniture except what's in her bedroom.

Jessica, all I could think was *Jessica*. I'm just seeing it. I'm seeing that it begins with the spirits ... that they're the centre of it.

I told Clarke he couldn't include it in the Passe Muraille season without your consent. Somewhere around the time when I was starting to make it concrete, I had to talk to Thompson. I told him what I was doing, but we couldn't connect, the thing was already out of his domain. It was on paper now, it had passed over to me or maybe you would say I'd taken it.... Anyway, there was no way we could talk about it as if it was still a collaboration. After Paul left that night, I was in tears again, I wanted to stop, to give up.

I didn't know how you would react. I'm, like, in this haze, where I'm writing a play that might never be done. Then Clarke started reading what I was doing, giving comments, encouraging me. All the time, I'm in a state. It was just this endless, fucking tangle. In my guts I knew I should do it, but nothing else made sense, nothing. Then you sent that card, and I called you on the phone and you said you were angry, that you were even angrier at Paul, and I didn't even know that you were that angry at Paul. Devastated again, I thought 'Fuck. How is this ever going to get done? This is impossible.'

But I couldn't stop. It was the first time I had ever written completely by myself, and I found I could finally handle the loneliness. Buried in piles of paper, I came across Maria's version of an ancient story, the legend of the White Buffalo Calf Woman. The story tells of a woman who comes from the spirit world, to bring the pipe to the people and teach them the prayers and songs. Two men see her walking along the prairie, one wants to rape her and is turned to dust, the other sees she is a holy woman and leads her to the camp. After she teaches the people, she walks away, becomes a huge white buffalo calf, then turns to stone.

MARIA   That's what these guys forget now, when they want to go back to the old ways. It was a woman that brought the pipes, that taught the prayers. They want to forget all about that part. But, the grandmothers won't let them....

Much later, I would sit with Maria at her kitchen window, listening to her talk about the unexplored white side of *Jessica*. I looked out to opposite side of the river bank, and out of the corner of my eye saw what looked like a white shadow. I didn't want to admit it, but I knew what it was. 'Oh, no, not a unicorn.' But I couldn't get her out of my mind. From my fatal faerie tale past, a unicorn. Not exactly the ethereal imagining of my adolescent bedroom, but a wild, primal kind of creature, born before realism, with a different kind of romantic's beauty. As if she'd gotten kicked out of China, ended up in Mesopotamia, had her run in Babylon, got chased north to Gaul, captured in some medieval tapestries, fled to old Ireland, snuck on a boat to the New World, became enshrined in the knickknack corner of Woolworth's, and ended up across the Saskatchewan River, saying, 'Don't you think there's a reason you're so fascinated by me?' I thought people would laugh at me if I put a unicorn in *Jessica*, but what could I do? She just walked into that play, the weirdest mixed frequency of all, as if she belonged with the 'real' animal presences of Crow, Coyote, Wolverine and Bear; as if in answer to the White Buffalo Calf Woman; as if in answer to the question, 'How does this goddess stuff fit in?' Maria laughed, not exactly with derision, but with that twisted sense of humour.

After the Fact

Just as I had finished a new first draft of *Jessica*, a friend bumped into Maria in Banff, telling her I was laid up. I received a card from her, picturing a very pale Lady of Shallot, floating down a river in waves of yellow hair. It was definitely a gesture of reconciliation. I was ecstatic, then terrified, spending days trying to word an answer, afraid of offending her again, still not understanding what the original offense had been, knowing that whatever she'd said on the phone that day, if I told her I had already written a draft she'd have a definite negative reaction. Instead, I wrote that I wanted us to work on *Jessica* again, that if she wasn't interested in an actual writing process, her approval would be necessary for anything to be presented or performed. Later I thought if she did want to work on it, I'd show her what I'd done and see what she said.

Months passed. No reply from Maria. Meanwhile, Jessica was out of her crate, sitting on the side of my bed, pulling at my sleeve, invading my dreams. I wrote a second draft and just sent it to Maria, still thinking of it as a kind of proposition, something on paper to get a concrete response, any response. No answer. Finally I called her, and the call was a horrible echo of the conversation in

Saskatoon. Again, she told me she was very angry. I can still feel what that word from her did to me, a cringing feeling, it still does it to me; anger as a whip to protect something valuable, and often exploited; anger as a way of stopping the project, any time, at any stage. Once more she felt betrayed. I was almost ready to get angry back, to stand my ground, but instead I found myself again defending the words on paper as a starting place, not a *fait accompli*. But suddenly, standing in my living room so far away from her, I knew what she knew, that this time it was a lie. What I had sent her was more than a proposition, it was the play. Right or wrong, I'd taken for myself the rights of half a Halfbreed, and had written it as it came. But I didn't dare say that to her, I didn't dare.

MARIA   I was working on a screenplay at the Banff Centre, when this woman tells me that you're all crippled up, and that Paul had a car accident and his daughter Sevrin just about died. Well, if you don't think I didn't go into a damn guilt thing! All of that negative energy I'd sent out! All of the horrible things I was going to do. But those were the two things I would never have even thought about.... Right away, I could hear Hannah telling me, I could hear my grandmother telling me, 'Think carefully before you say or think things. Be responsible, because the energy you put out can hurt others, and will come back to you. Power, energy, works in circles.' Then 'What have I done? I've put a curse on them.... I didn't mean to, but now Linda's all crippled up.... And then I remembered the time I saw that thing on your back. This sounds very....

LINDA   No. Not to me at all. Listen, nothing about *Jessica* sounds too weird. Believe me.

MARIA   I thought, 'I've put a curse on them. I wasn't being careful about the things I thought, and all that ugly stuff I walked around with for three months, walking back and forth in the snow, screaming at everything.... I'd done it, I'd hurt you. But I would never have thought of hurting a child or of crippling somebody. I might think of taking them to court and dragging them all over the newspapers, but not those kind of things.... Oh, Linda, you have no idea how upset I was.

    So I wrote you that letter. I didn't know what to do about Paul, because my rage and anger had been directed at Paul, but now it ended up with Sevrin ...? I didn't know how to

write and say, 'I'm sorry.' So I didn't. It turned out that Sevrin
was okay, but still, I didn't know how to deal with it. Then
you wrote me a letter back, so I was quite comfortable with
you. Then along comes the play, with you saying, 'Here it is.
Will you look at it?' And then my head ... it wasn't inside ... it
was my head that just blew up, and I thought, 'What in the
hell is she doing? She's saying, 'I want to work with you,' on
the one hand, and what she does is send me a written script.
What am I supposed to do after the fact? I got angry again,
then I thought, 'Okay, this time I'm going to tell her why I'm
angry and get it out.' I remembered Bear in ceremonies telling
me, 'Anger is okay as long as you don't keep it. Talk it out,
then you can learn to laugh and be happy.' So I wrote you a
long, long letter, but I never mailed it. I still have it
somewhere. Do you want to see it?

LINDA No. No no no no.

Back to Batoche

More months passed. Then Clarke, Paul, and some other Passe
Muraille people traveled west for 'Back to Batoche Days,' an
annual Metis celebration of the Battle of Batoche. It was the biggest
event ever, the hundredth anniversary (1885-1985). About a hundred people stayed with Maria at The Crossing, Gabriel Dumont's
homestead, in pitched tents along the river. It was the first contact
in all that time. I just waited.

MARIA Then along comes Clarke, and not long after, Thompson. And
I thought, 'Yeah, Thompson, you really know how to play me.
You come in '85, you know it's going to be full of people, so
I'm not going to have a confrontation with you. And you also
come to the place where you and I started.' You see, I always
associated Paul with The Crossing and Batoche, I never could
separate him from the place. Well, we said hello and we chit-
chatted, but there was this thing between us: The Process. I
had a hard time with him, he was so good. Paul was never
that kind to me before, he was always challenging me,
pushing. But during that time at Batoche, he was so gentle. He
was just like the grandfather, coming home, looking after the
people, talking to them, sitting back and having long

conversations. And then he was gone. So we never talked about it.

In the meantime, I worked like a dog with the Batoche committee, to make sure no exploiters could get in and do, you know, that 'Oh, here's some Canadian history for somebody's coffee table' kind of thing. And when Paul came, I thought about that. But I didn't stop him. It just seemed natural that he should be there, even if I didn't want him there.

And Clarke, he was like one of the kid brothers that had come home for the celebration, as if he'd always been there, as if he'd been born and raised there, and he hauled water and got groceries....

Something happened a couple of days before they left – and this is the most uncanny thing. I mean, Thompson really is magic sometimes, that's why he spooks me. My daughter and I were walking around on the grounds and we saw this display of guns. They were for sale. I mean, I am not a gun collector, but as we were walking by, Roxanne spotted it first, a special edition of Gabriel's old buffalo hunting gun, a perfect copy. I picked it up, I wanted it. I said, 'Wouldn't that look great hanging over the kitchen door?' We asked the guy what the price was and it was over a thousand dollars. There was no bloody way. We didn't have any money. A thousand dollars would buy us groceries for a year, so I said, 'If Uncle Gabe wants it hanging in his house, we'll get it.'

The next day, Thompson came in with all of his guys, and they're looking, like, you know.... They walk in and they stand in the living room. I was visiting with some people. Thompson really directed it, everybody looked at them, at all these guys standing there, beaming, like brothers. He's got this big envelope in his hand, and he said, 'This is for you. We think it would look really great hanging in here.' I opened it up and it was this gun. I started to cry. Roxanne was sleeping, I woke her up and showed her, and she started to cry too.

LINDA So Roxanne wasn't in on it?

MARIA No.

LINDA So, he overheard you?

MARIA No. He didn't know anything about it. When I asked, 'How did you know?,' he said, 'We saw it and thought it would look great hanging over the kitchen door.' And he pointed to the very spot.... So when Thompson left, it was like, he did it to me again.

It was Clarke who spoke directly to Maria about *Jessica*, the new script, and got her to talk about what had happened in Saskatoon. He drew her fire. Thompson's presence did the rest.

Finally, I received another card from Maria. It said, 'No matter what's happened, we're still sisters. Come on out to The Crossing and we'll talk.'

I traveled with my script in my hand. As I got off the plane, I kept saying to myself, 'Don't get speedy, don't talk too much, listen to the silences, just pretend you're ... a Native person – "brown up." ' I looked up, and there was Maria. We embraced carefully, aware that each of us was a little bit fragile.

It was only the beginning....

LINDA I'm still holding back on stuff about me, it's hard for me to tell things that are personal....

MARIA I know.... I can see you censoring yourself. But if we're going to do this ... this healing, this telling of the story, you have to get it out. I don't need to write a book.

LINDA I think you do.

MARIA Maybe, but this is different. I've already written my book, and I'm still feeling the repercussions, but when it came out it was a healing for me. That's what has to happen with you.

LINDA I'm trying, Maria.

MARIA Because if you don't talk, do something about it, then I can't do anything about my stuff. Linda, we're stuck to each other like Siamese twins....

LINDA I know, Maria, I know....

MARIA So can we stick this in with the story of the rehearsals and all that?

LINDA I think this is still the story of the rehearsals, the story of the rehearsals never ends....

The Red Cloth

The Argument. June 1988, Toronto

MARIA   Every time I get a letter from you or a phone call, or I turn the answering machine on and it's Linda, I think 'Oh ... no.' Anyway, I started reading this manuscript and halfway through it, I thought, 'Not again, I'm starting to feel angry, a sense of losing. What am I reading this for, because what I have to say is not going to make a difference anyway. She's going to do it the way she wants. She's going to make changes ... and she'll do it any way she can, by crying ... getting crippled up....

LINDA   Whatever happens....

MARIA   Whatever happens, she's going to manipulate it, and then, if I don't like it, I have to go through this whole scene again, being the bad guy, telling her, ' Linda, that's not what I want to do, and you've taken some of my stuff out of context.' Remember the cat getting hit story?

LINDA   Yeah.

MARIA   Because that was the first story that came to me and I....

LINDA   That's partly my story ... with the cat....

MARIA   But I mean the story I told you originally....

LINDA   Oh....

MARIA   I thought, 'I'm going to write down one thing that I told her that I can remember in detail, the way I told her.' So, I wrote it all down, and then I got finished and I thought, 'But what's the point of me sitting down and writing anything? She's going to pay no attention to it.'

LINDA   Maria ... but that's exactly what I want you to do.

MARIA   No it isn't, but it does work better when we talk....

LINDA   Yeah.

MARIA   Because when it's written, it just sounds too ... it sounds written.

LINDA   I mean, I've been doing....

MARIA   So, anyway, let me finish. So, what ends up happening

67

is that I get myself in a ... I mean, this thing happens to me. I know you're going to be all uptight about something when I arrive. You know. I could really feel you vibing me on Saturday. My period started, and it was really bad, so I didn't feel like getting up. I didn't want to see you, I didn't want to see anybody. So there I was, trying to block you out, and I thought, 'Well, I should phone.' And then I thought, 'What for, she's going to phone pretty soon,' and sure enough, you called. And I thought 'I don't want to do this fucking thing again, this is just about eight years now.... Why don't I just go home?' I do this every time, Linda, really get myself worked up, and then it's like we start setting ourselves up so that everything will be a crisis or a conflict. Anyway, I arrived here last night. I knew you weren't going to be home, and....

LINDA You said you were coming at 1:30.

MARIA I knew you weren't going to be home and I knew you were going to be uptight, I opened the door and walked in and I just knew. Everything is all clean and I thought, 'Oh, yeah. Sure. She cleaned house, what else?' Then I remembered I'd said to you once that I've got to have potatoes and meat, so I opened up the fridge and there was this big pot and I thought, 'Fuck.' I opened it up and there they are, potatoes and meat. 'She's laying a guilt trip on me, I'm supposed to feel guilty because the house is all clean, and there's food in the fridge.' I sort of walked around for a while, and then I thought, 'To hell with it, I'm hungry,' so I warmed it up.

LINDA [*laughing*] That's too good....

MARIA I mean, it was just crazy! Then I went and sat outside, and the cat sat with me, and I thought, 'Ahh, what am I getting myself all worked up about?' So I started writing, 'Why am I doing this?'

LINDA Right.

MARIA Am I doing it for money? No. Linda says it's cost her money. This has cost me money, too.

LINDA Yes.

MARIA There's been a lot of conflict and pain in my life too, pain that's turned me inside out because of this stupid play. You know, every time I look at it, it does all kind of weird things to me. So.... Okay. It's not for the money. And then, five pages later, I still don't have an answer. So then I asked, 'Do I want something from you? Is there something that you've got that I want?'

LINDA Why would....

MARIA For me, there has to be a reason why I do something. I worked with Paul because I wanted to learn the process ... there has to be a reason.

LINDA Umhmm.

MARIA Okay. My reason for doing anything, is that it's for my community. I am a community worker, the work has to be useful to the community, has to be healing. So when I look at this work from that point of view, I don't see it as healing to the community, at least not the way it is. So I think 'Okay. If I really am a community worker, then I'm not being as responsible as I should be. I'm not being as honest ... because I don't want to hurt you. We've had this argument before ... in fact, we had one the other night.... It's about the swearing, the blatant sexuality, all that stuff. You and I are really different in how we see that. Healing – and for me that's theatre, writing – is that you try to find ... you find what's beautiful, the essence, and that's what you give back. You know what I mean? That's community work. Some of those scenes in *Jessica* make my hair stand up on end. I don't understand why we have to be so explicit....

LINDA Yes.

MARIA I know that there has to be ...

LINDA ... a story with a truth.

The Virgin Mary Again. January 1988, Saskatoon

LINDA I still feel it, like you could get angry any minute. I feel like I've still got my hands up to protect me. I didn't understand why you were angry, didn't even know that you were angry most of the time, certainly not that angry.

MARIA You don't know what a love/hate relationship it's
been with you, you don't know. You'd stand there
with this smile on your face, just stand there wanting
more. So innocent, so nice. Like a bloody virgin being
raped by all these men and you didn't even know it.
Paul even, all of them. And you just wanted me to
give you more. You didn't know anything. And I
would get so angry. I'd see you and I'd see the
Catholic Church, and my mother kneeling for hours in
front of that statue with that nice innocent face. She
wanted to be nice like that. If she hadn't of wanted to
be nice like that, she would have been able to love me,
but she couldn't, because I wasn't nice, I was never
nice like that, I was always angry, as far back as I can
remember. I'd see you, with that stupid Virgin face,
and I'd think of what they did to us, stole from us, all
our strength, making us look like that, like you, with
your glassy stare. You were the Church, and men, and
white people, and cops, and rules, and you'd come
out with these phrases, these little phrases like a
machine, and I knew where you got those phrases,
from 'them.' You were a product. And I'd think, 'You
and Paul are laughing at us, you don't believe in any
of this, this isn't even a play to you, it's just a joke.'
Then I'd be defending you to my friends, saying, 'You
think they stole from us, our strength, our culture, the
mother, all of it, but look what they stole from her. She
never got any of that teaching, not like we did, it
happened to us only a hundred years ago, it happened
to them thousands of years ago.' And then you'd get
up there and stuff would come out of your mouth,
you'd move in certain ways and I'd see my younger
self, just like I was, and I'd hate you for it. Then you'd
be there again, wanting more.
　　There's a grotto near Batoche, called St. Laurent,
one of those Lourdes kind of Catholic places with a
statue of the Mother. When we were rehearsing, Paul
wanted us to go there. 'Go there? To that place with
that smarmy statue, go to a place stolen from us, with
their simpy version of woman?' But the best berries in

the area grow there. There's something about the Church and berries.... Anyway, I would go there berry picking, but I wouldn't look at the grotto, I'd just grit my teeth and pass by. After you came to visit, before the Toronto production, I went there all by myself to go berry picking, but I think I really wanted to look at 'her.' So I walked down the hill and I started to get this really good feeling, like it was okay. When I got to the statue, I looked at her face. There she was in her robes, with that innocent face, and I didn't hate her anymore, I didn't even feel sorry for her. I understood her. I felt she'd been kept alive at least. I put some tobacco out for her. Now I like to go there often.

LINDA It was the only way I could protect myself, with innocence, niceness. I just couldn't figure out why anyone would want to get mad at someone who was trying so hard. I'm angry too, but it's never directed out. I changed it into theatre energy, or I turned it inside. What would have happened if I'd fought you? Then you could have given up, quit the whole thing, but you couldn't, you couldn't fight what I was putting out. Like a blank page staring at you. It was the only way it could have happened. Like a science-fiction mind transplant in which only one of the people knows it's happening. The other one thinks she knows, but she doesn't. Maybe neither of them know. The mad scientist doesn't know either, he just dreams up the machinery and switches it on, hoping it'll make a nice hit play and we won't get fried in the process. I thought, 'She's looking at me, thinking I've had all this privilege, this education, thinking what she would have done if she'd been given what I had.' She's thinking, 'All that privilege, to produce this wimpy girl.' I thought you were jealous of what I could do with your material, your life. You hated having to use me to get it out. I was ashamed to be me in front of you. You were better, braver, more real than me, but you couldn't do what I could do. My only protection was my innocence, my little white hand on your arm – 'Maria, why are you angry? Why don't you like me?' –

hating myself for the smile on my face. But you did talk to her, that girl with the smile. For some reason you gave her what you couldn't give anyone else, not lovers, family, children, community. And somewhere I know that little white hand was buried right in your guts, saying, 'Give it to me, I know where to put it, trust me.' You'd never survived in suburbia, you didn't understand that kind of warfare, that kind of warrior, the one in a pink dress and Mary Janes.

MARIA So, what are we going to do?

LINDA We're going to do this bloody book, or whatever.

MARIA How?

LINDA We'll figure it out.

The Devil

MARIA But why? Okay, the first time it was your job, you were the actress, or whatever, and it was set up for me to give you all my stuff, and for you to.... But why did we go so far? And what about now? Why are you doing this, what's in it for you? It can't just be one way anymore Linda, you have to show me something ...

LINDA ... you know why I didn't want to go into all your Catholic stuff in *Jessica*? Because my mother had just cured herself by going right into the Catholic religion. I couldn't put that down when she'd just saved her own life. She's like me, you think she's going to buckle under it all, then she comes back with this really tough self.

MARIA I get so mad. I control it better now, but I get so angry. I'm a storyteller from an oral tradition, but the language ... my language isn't even English, so when I go to write about ... about that stuff ... I just can't. Maybe it's because I'm not educated ... I don't know.... I've got grade seven, but it's like grade three, because the teachers hardly knew more than we did. But when I'd sit down and try to write the ... deeper ... complicated stuff, I knew I'd have to use 'him.' I'd feel the conqueror, the oppressor, making me use his language, and I knew I'd never use it as well as him

and I'd feel so powerless, and think, 'They stole
everything, and now we can't just speak any more, the
old language is almost gone and we don't know the
new language well enough to help each other, heal
each other ... we're just hanging there in the middle.'
And I feel him down deep inside, taking things from
women, from our people, taking things that we are
supposed to give our babies. His way is 'power over'
– and I hate.... Then I think, 'What is that hate, what is
it?' Is it enough to say, 'They did it to us? They took
everything away?' What about us? Surely we weren't
that stupid. Am I saying I'm from a people that are
stupid? I mean, we weren't raped right away, they
didn't come off those ships and steal and rape
immediately, there was some bartering that went on.
Was it greed that my people felt? Was that how they
got sucked in? It's like the matriarchies – what
happened? They came into the matriarchies and took
it all away, and suddenly we had nothing. It happened
so quickly, it didn't take thousands of years. And I
think, 'Was it this evil force? Not men, really, but ...
some kind of evil. Or did we do it to ourselves?'

LINDA   We did it to ourselves.

MARIA   When you first said that, I wanted to hit you. I hated
you saying that. So pat – 'We did it to ourselves' –
without thinking of all the suffering that's been
caused....

LINDA   I did think of it. But whenever I read those feminist
books about the goddess, I always feel like they're
side-stepping something. 'There was this perfect time
in the matriarchy and then the bad men came along
and ruined it.' I just can't buy it. How did we lose
what we had?

MARIA   I just didn't want to hear it. Then I thought, but why,
why did we do it? Did we just give up, like my
mother?

LINDA   We got tired and we handed it over, it was too hard.
We gave it to men....

MARIA   Well, I don't know. It's hard to believe they took it
themselves, they're not bright enough to think of that

themselves.... But what is that hate, what is it that makes humans destroy? What made the men destroy the very thing that made them strong, because when they put us down, they put themselves down, devoured their own power and turned themselves into babies.

LINDA If you're Catholic, you call it the Devil.

MARIA I know. It's so simple.

LINDA It's just a way to call it. I call it fear.

MARIA But people have seen the Devil. I was out at The Crossing one night, trying to write, and I was feeling this ... this anger, this hate and it was like a physical thing, and it was frightening me. So I went outside in the middle of the night and I thought, 'Okay, people have called you before, they've wanted to see you, they've seen you, so come on, I want to see you.'

I was scared, but I was so tired of feeling this way, feeling this thing, that I did it, I really did want to see him, talk to him, at least I could ask why ... whatever. I started walking along the river, trying to conjure him up, and all of a sudden I could feel him, like this dense ball of energy the size of a grapefruit ... ooh and it was ugly. I started running for my life along the river, I was terrified ... I could feel it at my back so close, inches from my spine and it was chasing me. I'm thinking, 'Why did I do this at night, with no cars on the highway? Why didn't I do it in the circle in front of the house, why did I do it with no protection? Why did I do it at all?' Finally I whipped around to face it. I wasn't brave, I didn't turn around slowly and do it with dignity, it was like, 'Here goes nothing, it can't be worse than it is now,' and as I turned to face it, it was gone, just disappeared, there was nothing, only the night. I walked back and I saw the house, with the one bulb shining in front of it. I saw the circle of stones in front, and I thought of what I'd been told: 'Why are you so afraid of being alone? We come into this world alone, and we go out alone, there's nothing wrong with that.' I looked up at the stars and thought, 'But you guys, you're are all together.' And something

happened, it was like 'ping!' The stars moved, or
something moved, my sight perhaps, and for the first
time I saw that each star was separate, each one alone,
and I felt their aloneness, completely, for the first time.
I really felt what it was to be alone, and it was alright.

But why, Linda? Why are you doing this now?
What do you want from me? What did you want then
and what do you want now? I have to know.

LINDA It has to do with pain. I didn't have anger, I've still
barely have found it. I had pain, but how could I say I
had pain? I needed someone ... someone who had felt
tangible pain ... it was so clear with you, a life filled
with racism, with oppression, lived against horrible
odds just pressing you down. How could I speak
about my own pain? All my life I'd been told I had it
good – white, two parents, a nice home, only two kids
in the family, two cars ('not new ones,' as my father
always said, but two cars); a decent education, no
trouble about food, no beatings, no overt violence.
How could I say what I felt? That I was in terrible pain
for whatever reason, maybe for no reason? Then my
back seizes up and I start going backwards. I went
into my past, and saw a different kind of violence.
Everything repressed under the dining room table. It's
amorphous, like air; you go to hit it and it gives up,
you go to name it and it curls up in a nice ball like a
kitten, you yell at it and it cries. You say, 'How could
you do this to me?,' and you're looking at two loving
parents who tried to do their best. You can't find it. It's
like coming from a shopping mall, and that's your
culture. Nothing worse happened than shopping at
Simpsons, but underneath Simpsons, underneath the
ground the shopping mall is on, are lies and fears and
horrors nobody knows. You grew up with spooky
stories, part Indian, part Catholic, part ghost stories of
banshees, spirits and devils. I grew up desperate for
stories that would fit my nightmares, but there
weren't any, so you deny the nightmares, hide them.
Even the Catholicism I got was soft-core.

When I started to ... act you ... write you ... whatever

it was I did ... I could act the way I felt, as if
somewhere I had been beaten, raped, oppressed. I
could act from the part of me that wasn't a nice clean
girl, the girl inside me that was huddled in a corner,
who wanted to destroy herself because she hurt so
much, and no one would listen because it looked so
good on the outside. I couldn't speak of her then, but
when I heard your story, there was finally a reason to
act the way I felt. I protected myself the way middle-
class women do. You can't fight that, you can't hit it.
Why would you punch me?

MARIA Well ... people love to punch me. To punch you would
be like hitting a cloud.

LINDA I have a lot of violence in me. At times Passe Muraille
has been a really brawling place. It's made me feel
terrible, but I've liked it as well. Being involved with
you, with the way you're not afraid to get mad, or
never speak to anyone again, or....

MARIA But you made me feel so ... dirty.... I don't know when
I stopped being innocent. I think when I was really
young, I got hard, or practical, or jaded. You were the
person my mother wanted me to be. Watching you in
those improvs, I felt like an old whore, bitter and
marked, and there you were with your pure face. I
wanted to kick you and hold you at the same time.

LINDA I didn't know.

MARIA I know you didn't know, that's what made me so mad.
Then when stuff would happen.... I wanted to say it
was because you were white, but I knew it wasn't
true, I couldn't deny you ... I wanted to protect you,
and that made me madder.

LINDA But why would you want to be mad at a nice girl like
me?

MARIA Exactly, and that made me madder. Much later, I
began to realize I couldn't turn my back on all that
Catholic stuff, because most of my people are
Catholics, well, sort of Catholics, and I began to
understand the Old Woman, the Virgin and the
Mother. Really, not from my head, but deep inside.
There you were the Virgin, and there I was, the

Mother, and I could also see the old woman I would
be.... Look at the lights.

LINDA What lights?

MARIA The lights....

LINDA Here in the kitchen? ... Maria don't scare me.... You
mean like little particles in the sunlight?

MARIA Sort of.

LINDA I can't see them, Maria. I can sort of see them ... but not
... really....

Bag of Rocks

MARIA The relationship I've had with you in the last eight
years has helped me to see the white part of myself.
And part of the obsession for me to stay here is
because I want you to see it too – which is really hard
to explain, because I feel that your 'self' is not in the
Indian part of me. When I was reading what you said
about your feeling guilty about what's been done to
Native people, well, you can feel bad about that, but
that's your history too. That's the white part of you.
That's your history. That happened to you, to your
people. You've got to feel angry about that as well....
Sometimes, I feel really bizarre, weird, you know, like
I'm your mother. Other times, I feel like you're my
mother and I'm the kid. Other times, I think it's like
the relationship I had with Hannah.

LINDA But the white part of you knows exactly how I feel
when you don't show up.

MARIA Don't pressure me with these things. You know I'm
not very good with time. In fact, I'm totally unreliable.
The way I feel about time or appointments is not the
same way you feel about them. I respect and
appreciate that those things are important to you, but
they're just not very important to me. You know, like,
if you were to come along and take the stuff that I
picked up at the second-hand store and crap all over it
or something, I could understand that, because that's
important to me, but not time. I'm always here when

you really need me.... I don't understand about time, stealing, yes, but not the importance you put on it.... Time – what is that anyway?

LINDA It has nothing to do with appointments. It has to do with respect – basic respect. I thought what was happening was that finally, after all this time, we were finally respecting each other, and then you didn't show up again. I feel like I've single-handedly kept this thing together so that there would be something, which is very important to me because I do consider myself a writer and always, all my life, I've been attached to ... I don't know ... accomplishing things ... 'accomplishment' doesn't sound right ... that things would exist, the creation of things. That so much energy, so much pain, so much creativity, so much love, hate, tears, blood, could be spent on the production of *Jessica* that we originally did, and that it could die completely ... it's against something so deep in me that I know it comes ... I don't know ... I could say it comes from my ancestors, or from the spirits or whatever you want to call it, but it runs deep, deep inside.

MARIA Umhmm....

LINDA I just feel like a water diviner. I go in with my whale bone thing and I feel heat or I feel energy. I feel I've driven this book, bullied it, willed it. I have taken unbelievable amounts of shit from you and an absolute lack of respect. And just when I think that there's absolutely nothing coming from you, you switch around and are so wonderful that I feel awful for having ever doubted that you were there. The switching always wrecks me. I get all worked up, and then I see you and think, 'What am I worked up about? This woman is dedicated to the same things I am.' But you're not dedicated in the same way, because you would have let *Jessica* die.

MARIA You think I would have.

LINDA Yes. I feel like I take the bag of rocks and drag it up the fucking hill, saying, 'Maria, this bag of rocks is partly your idea. Where are you?,' and then you're not there.

And then, just when I'm about to say, 'Fuck this bag of rocks,' you're just there and....

MARIA But I've always been there.

LINDA Yeah?

MARIA You can't say that I would have let it die, because you don't know that.

LINDA No, I don't know that.

The Treaty

LINDA To use Wolverine, the wolverine in me said ... 'I have the power to write that play and it will not be written the way I want unless I do it.' That's it. I felt that it would be watered down, or never happen, or take forever. I couldn't write it with you because I felt that it would be too hard. Look how hard it is seven years later, it would have been impossible then. Wolverine just said, 'Give it to me, because I can do something with it.'

MARIA And the Bear asks, 'Why do you need me then? Why do you come back? Why do you come back if you're that positive about it?'

LINDA And the Coyote says, 'Because it's not entirely one thing or the other, because it is not my culture, and because you're involved and it would be dishonourable for me to take it without your involvement and blessing.' I gave you veto power, remember or not. But, at the same time, I know there was enormous pressure on you not to use that power. On the phone that day you said, 'Take the play. I don't care what you do with it. Do whatever you want with it.' I had that phrase ringing in me and I thought, 'She doesn't care about this project as much as I do.'

MARIA But you set her up to say that.

LINDA No. In Saskatoon I was an actress. I was in the middle of it. I had no fucking idea what was going on. I knew so much less than you and Paul about what was happening, that it's frightening. I was simply within it. I called you up to say, 'Good-bye Maria. It's been amazing. We'll work on it in a couple of months when we both have time.' Instead I get, 'I never want to see you and Paul again. You can take the bloody thing and do whatever the hell you want with it.'

MARIA So what you're saying is that the play lived, period. It's done very well and it wouldn't have if you hadn't done it.

LINDA Yes. That's what I'm saying.

MARIA So I'm asking, why was it important for me to be a part of it after it was written?

LINDA Okay. Pure Wolverine, I needed you.

MARIA What did you need me for?

LINDA You gave lots of comments on that script. I took everything you said.

MARIA If you thought you were doing the right thing, why did you have to come back to me then?

LINDA Because it wasn't entirely me.

MARIA Then Wolverine wasn't that sure.

LINDA Okay. If Wolverine does whatever is necessary to get the kill, or to do the thing, then I needed your input for it to be accomplished. I needed you to take it apart and say what you thought was false and true. And I also needed for myself to ... not to steal from you. It's like this unbelievable catch-22. I did not steal from you because the creation is both of us, but the action was mine.

MARIA Now Wolverine is saying, 'I took it. I gave it birth. I gave it life. It was mine and it would have died without me. I salvaged it. I built temples all over the place. I built high-rises all over the place. I put wheat fields out there. I produced it and if it wasn't for me, you would have let this land die. So I came along and I took what you were wasting and I made something productive out of it, because you weren't doing it, but I need you to tell me that I didn't steal anything, that I didn't take anything from you.' So, if I tell you, 'No, Linda. You didn't take anything and, really, I support this,' then you can go home feeling okay, because then, if somebody questions it, you can say, 'Maria supports this.'

LINDA It wasn't just support though....

MARIA   I had a choice. And I made the choice. If I'd have come at it like Wolverine, I would have demolished you. But what I would have done was demolish somebody that couldn't fight with me.

LINDA   I can speak for Wolverine now, but then I couldn't. But it's not just your blessing, Maria. Your comments, your criticisms....

MARIA   But Linda, how can I make you understand? That's no different than the man in Ottawa who writes out the Indian Act, then comes to the people after it's done and asks for their blessing and input. Out of five thousand words, there might be five hundred that are good, but the others are going to hurt them over a period of years. And then he's upset because no one is gung-ho, hurt because no one appreciates....

LINDA   No. No. You started the project. I didn't. You started the energy and then, as far as I could tell, you were willing to kill it.

MARIA   The Wolverine part of you knew that I wasn't going to kill it. When you started rewriting, Linda, if you really think about it....

LINDA   As far as I knew, you had no interest in the play. You never wanted to see me or Paul again. 'Take the play.' That's what you said. How would you have me interpret that? Then you never contacted me. What was I supposed to think? And now you want to get after me for taking what you threw away in anger. But what I knew you had interest in was the energy that blessed the play. That's what really gave me the courage to pick it up again. All the time I was writing on my own I had a hatchet over my head. I thought, 'I have to accept that if Maria says 'No' ... then I will not do this play.' I have gone through hell and high water for this project because I believe it's blessed in some way. You told me it was.

MARIA   Of course it is. But talk about hell and high water – you've gone through hell and high water writing it, because of what you think I've done to you, but I go through hell and high water with that play every time it comes up, my family goes through hell and high water. Those are parts of our lives being played out. It means that all of that stuff is opened up again, over and over and over again. Don't talk to me about the kind of hell and high water you go through. You don't have a monopoly on that.

LINDA Neither do you.... You can make this great analogy that I'm the white guy in Ottawa saying, 'Here's a treaty,' but *Jessica* ... it's just hitting me now ... maybe *Jessica* is a treaty. To me, it was a sacred thing.

MARIA A treaty is a sacred thing, but a treaty has to be two equals, two people sitting down and respecting what the other one has to offer, and two people doing it together, negotiating. Otherwise, it's not a treaty.

LINDA All the logic, all the sociology and all the politics you could bring to it doesn't answer why this treaty is going on now. When Native people see *Jessica*, they don't say, 'Oh. This is a white person's view.' And yet it's dealing with things in the innermost corner of the culture, and I think the only way that happened was not just because of everything you gave me ... but because ... my spirits are your spirits. I don't know how else to say it.

Stealing

MARIA You can't be honourable if you are a thief.

LINDA I think....

MARIA If you are telling me you're not stealing, and on the other hand you are telling me you are being honourable, then I think, 'Well, what the fuck do you know about honour if you can't even admit you're a thief?'

LINDA They say there is honour among thieves.

MARIA Of course there is honour among thieves. But you have to first admit you are a thief.

LINDA Yes. That's what I am doing.

MARIA And you have to....

LINDA Right now. I'm admitting I'm a thief.

MARIA I know. Well, I mean....

LINDA I am. I'm a thief. I'm a fucking thief. I don't care, I have always been a thief.

MARIA But there is nothing wrong in that, as long as you know and accept.... We think we don't keep learning from Paul, but we do.

LINDA I know.

MARIA Remember when I told you one time, 'Paul comes in and steals the family jewels.' You started to cry when I told you that you guys came in and you stole. I was told that Paul would come in and he would find your family jewels, and he would walk off with them, and you wouldn't know they were gone until after. And you just went to pieces over that, and ran through whole reams and reams of stuff, about how you didn't steal, and you went on and on about honour, because 'honour' always comes up when we are talking about stealing.... I mean, I'm a storyteller, a writer....

LINDA Yeah.

MARIA Those are my ... the tools that I use. I also know, and I've told you over and over again, that I can't write unless I go into the community. You say, 'I'm an artist and I see my community as a global thing.' Well, fine, but to me that's bullshit.

LINDA I'm a thief. I'm not an artist. I'm a thief. And it's not just Native people I've stolen from. I've stolen from Margaret and Pierre Trudeau. I've stolen from the people that I met in Jamaica when we wrote *O.D. on Paradise*. I'm a professional thief.

MARIA That's what art is, Linda.

LINDA I've felt that you hated art.

MARIA But art has become a bad thing. I keep telling you that. Today, most art is ugly, because it's not responsible to the people it steals from. Real, honest-to-God true art steals from the people. It's a thief. It comes in. It's non-obstructive. You don't feel it. It comes in, and you don't even notice that it's there, and it walks off with all your stuff, but then it gives it back to you and heals you, empowers you, and it's beautiful. Seventy-five percent of the art that's out there steals, but it doesn't give anything back. It doesn't bring you joy. It doesn't heal you. It doesn't make you ask questions. It doesn't do anything. It takes your stuff and it hangs it up on the wall and it says, 'Look what I've done. Isn't that wonderful. I'm an artist.' It's all pure ego, and when you say that maybe I'm the healer and you're the artist, that's bullshit. If you're an artist and you're not a healer, then you're not an artist – not in my sense of what art is. Art is the most powerful ... it's the main healing tool. The artist in the old communities was the most sacred person of all.

LINDA That's how I've always felt, Maria.

MARIA Somewhere I must know that, or I wouldn't still be here.

More Stealing

LINDA I'm just like all the other white people, that's true. I'm a gold digger. I was then, and I still am. I couldn't believe it, Maria, it was like having a real faerie tale come true. I used to be nuts about faerie tales, but I had to stop because I was afraid it would drive me crazy, that I'd just wander away in my long nightgown into some wizard castle and never be heard of again. I was a nutcase. You talk about Tolkien, I've read the whole trilogy ten times. When I was nineteen years old, I had a doll that I dressed up as a princess, I coloured in colouring books, I read Grimm's and dreamed Arthur Rackham. But there was no politics in it, it was rarefied; there was no real fire, I was bloodless, it all felt bloodless, and I had to turn my back on it and come west to feel flesh and blood.

We began *Jessica,* and I started to feel that stuff again. When the Native world got opened up to me, it was like coming home. Here were people that believed the air was thick with things, like I did, that you could listen and hear voices. They believed in magic stones and passing through walls, they prayed to something or someone, but it wasn't like the Catholicism I couldn't believe in anymore, even though it never really left me. What I was learning felt clean. All those tired old images of horses and long dresses, and castles and wizards, and witches and wands, all those flogged-out symbols of magic we whites had beaten to death in our poems, songs, plays and movies, were all I had.

Then I saw your culture, and it was like a treasure chest opening up, and the maniac romantic in me just dived in up to my elbows. These images and stories were fresh, still alive, people still believed in them, they had real power. And I knew why my magic feelings had always been so transparent, because they weren't connected to prayer, as if magic and praying were two different things. And I knew why everything had always been so bloodless, because there was no struggle for realization in my airy feelings and worn-out images.

I am a gold digger. I went for that treasure chest with everything in me, my fists were full of your gold, my fingers closed in on your jewels. And if they were feathers and rocks, that didn't matter to me, and if the dancers and wizards lived in trailers and wore skidoo suits, that didn't bother me either. Somewhere I was at home, and I claim that home. You want to send me back to the druids, find strength in the dispossession of the Scots or the Celts, but I don't feel it. I was born here and the Native way is the way of the land here, right here where I was born. I know I was precious about it all, wanted to write everything. I had gold fever.

All my life I'd lived theatre, knowing it was meant to be spiritual, watching us try to make it that way with one tortured symbol. I've seen the Cross right side up, up side down, hung with plastic chickens, in Germany I saw a play where it was fucked. I've seen countless images on images, as if to call in the old Cross was the only way to reach out to our spirits. But the spirit of that Cross seemed to need a break. The Bible is the basis for just about everything in my culture, and I was tired of it, tired of the endless interpretations, tired of its view of women, hurt by the organized religions. But it was my only basis. When we tried to do the Greeks it always failed, because we didn't believe anything. Hell, we can hardly do Shakespeare, because we don't believe in ghosts, don't know anything about that world.

So I'm a gold digger. I was then and I am now. And it hurt so much then, and it hurts so much now, to see magic come alive and then have your wrists slapped because that magic can never be yours.

MARIA Nobody ever said the magic wasn't yours, that the power wasn't yours, nobody ever slapped your wrists, that was your interpretation of what you were being told. You just said that you were tired of interpreting all the interpretations of the Cross, all the witches, all the things that theatre and poetry had done to those images. All I was trying to tell you was that if you were tired of it, then why are you trying to do the same thing to us? Then one day the same thing will happen to our stuff, the same thing that happened to European culture. Remember what you said about the Cross and what the actors did to it in Germany. Do you want to see somebody fucking the stone on stage? We don't have gold magic anymore, gold doesn't do to the gold digger what it used to do, because someone saw that it was worth a fortune, because someone came along and exploited it, used it. They didn't mean to do that, they believed it had power, and that it would give them power, but what you have today is the flip side of the gold's power.

I can identify with finding stuff, and the incredible feeling, the rush it gives you, because my people have walked behind other cultures picking up things their parents discarded for generations: moral traditions, sacred things, songs, prayers, everything ... a way of tying a scarf, a jig step. When you look at what we have as mixed-blood people you see all these things woven into something that became a new nation. Maybe I get overly uptight when I tell you, 'Don't do that,' but it's only because, if we exploit it and don't even fully understand it ourselves, then we're giving something away to be abused.

The things you've just told me are showing me a person, you're letting me see you, you're talking to me. You're letting me see you as an equal with things inside.

When I say I saw the Virgin Mary, pure and empty, that's all I could see because you didn't give me anything else. I knew you had a mother and a father and a brother, that's all I knew. I'd come home after talking to you for hours and not feel you at all. And it has been like that until these last few days. Do you have any idea what you did for me when you told me you'd been a booster? I just about fell off my chair. You're freaking out now because someone might read this. Hey, she's real, she's been in conflict, she farts in the toilet too. Talk about not being able to feel me, because I was 'dignified,' well, you sure had me fooled. A booster ... wow ... a paperhanger, maybe, but I'd never have guessed.

LINDA If I'd have known it would get me so many points with you, believe me, I would have told you sooner. But that's the thing about Paul's work. We went into communities and acted out other people, sibyled them. But we, as emotional beings, weren't really a part of it. Paul was reacting against a whole dead area in our culture. Instead of talking to people, artists started imitating other artists, so that they become the whole point of things. And if you do that, you can ignore your own land completely, because you're too lazy or scared to find out how your people actually talk. But it was dangerous for me, because I really believed myself to be a medium, that I wasn't important. Not everybody who worked with Paul was like me, almost blank like that. I take things so literally, but I think ignoring the emotional lives of his actors became the Achilles' heel of his work.

When we brought the person to be explored into the room, it opened the door for there to be a relationship. I had to be a person to you. But I didn't really believe myself to be a person, certainly not an interesting person.

When you said that you wanted to work with Paul and me, I thought, 'Well, I can see why she wants to work with Paul, but why would she want to work with me? I could be anybody, I'm just the medium, like any other.' What happened in that rehearsal process was I couldn't get by with just being the sibyl, but I didn't know enough to be anything else. It broke me open. I've spent all these years, and the writing of *Jessica*, trying to connect up the inside with the outside, because I knew I couldn't continue the way I was anymore.

Faerie Glass

MARIA You started thinking, 'Oh God, my mother is going to read this.'

LINDA Yeah.

MARIA If you are going to talk about me and my community, if you really are a thief, and you really are an artist, you have to able to be as honest about yourself too. You can't lay something out, and then say, 'Well, I can't do that because it might hurt some people.' You can do it. But don't lay rules on me that you can't follow yourself. That's like me having a relationship with a man who says it's okay for him to screw around, but not for me. Why is it okay to lay my guts all over the table, but you can only take some of yours, and by the way, madam, let's make sure they're the pretty ones. I've had a hard time with this the last few years, you being so virginal. Don't ask me to do something that you're not prepared to do, and if you're not prepared to do it, then understand why I'm nervous about working with you.

LINDA I don't know if you are my 'dark mother' ... the mother that will really come after me, that's willing to be cruel. Maybe you are that for me. But I know that, somewhere, this has to do with me taking a bit of the faerie glass off my own eyes. Just like when you talk about me coming to you all crippled up, and I wonder, did I do all that to myself just to be able to do this play? Just so I would be unattackable?

MARIA And that's normal, natural. That's probably why I didn't wipe you out. Because there is this whole other relationship between us. There's a whole other part that had nothing to do with the play. Somewhere along the way, when I first started to learn, why wasn't there somebody else that I could have started to work with? Why did you come along? You were my first student.

LINDA Really?

MARIA Yeah, and then you became my teacher. You see, in order for me to be able to learn whatever it is I have to learn, I had to go through all this stuff. I had to be messed up, and crippled up and dying in order to be able to learn, to be able to pick up one little jewel from Hannah, or from somebody else. If I would have come strong and together and centred, I would have learned nothing. I remember how Hannah would just batter me around, or I thought she did, and make me so angry. I'd drag myself home, thinking, 'Well, I'm not going to have anything more to do with her. What the hell am I putting myself through this for?' But I would always come back. There were times I swore she hated me, didn't want me to know anything, and deliberately did things so I wouldn't know anything. But now I know I deliberately did things to myself so that I would be in bad shape when I came back. I've been able to understand her better in my relationship with you. Someone once said, 'When the student is ready, the teacher is there, so the teacher can learn.' Does that make sense?... It does to me.

 Why would you come to visit me strong and healthy? I wouldn't have given you anything. I would never have understood the relationship I had with Hannah without you. I never came to Hannah healthy and strong and together. Until I came with you.

 Before I ever met you I went to a ceremony to find out if I should do this play, and I was told, yes, it was okay as long as I thought it was okay. But I had to be sure it was right, because I was going to be responsible for whatever came out of this thing. I was

reminded in that ceremony, 'Whether you're a
storyteller, a painter ... whatever you are, you're a
healer first. Whatever you do with that, it will come
back one day. And if it's good energy, and it's healing,
it will heal you too. Remember that, and if you think
this is right, don't be afraid to let it go.'

LINDA Just know the responsibility.

MARIA Just know the responsibility. When you talk about
being frightened of me, I think, 'Well, what's she
frightened of me for? I mean, I should lay some of the
things on her that Hannah laid on me.' But then,
maybe I have, and I haven't been aware of it.

LINDA Well, it finds it's own level. Right?

MARIA Yeah.

The Brick

MARIA *Jessica* does have that kind of feeling ... like, if I walk
under a ladder, I know it's going to fall on me.

LINDA This brick is coming for my head. It doesn't matter
where I am, but it's going to fall on my head. We talk
about these things, and I think, 'There's nothing left to
be said about this experience.' And then there's still
something that hurts.

MARIA What do you think it is?

LINDA That I can never own it.

Owning

MARIA In community work there's an exchange of power, a
sharing, and as a result we all get strong. But what
I've learned from *Jessica* in the last little while ... why
do I hurt when we talk about these things? It's because
I can never own it either, and everything else in my
life I've always owned. I'm the one that gives ... and
once I learn to be generous ... because I don't think I'm
stingy anymore ... but maybe I am, because I won't let
go.

Why do I hurt when we talk about the play
especially, never mind the rest of the stuff. Where
does that come from? It's so hard ... the world is all

ownership, people owning land, houses, things, always accumulating. I don't believe that comes from my culture, from my community ... the influence, the essence comes from outside, we struggle with that influence constantly, our culture isn't one of ownership. Our elders teach us that we don't own, can never own the land, the stories, the songs, not in the way that the outside views ownership. Our culture believes in giving, potlatches and give-aways are all a part of the sacred circle. To grow spiritually, to be healthy physically, you have to let go, give away. But it's bloody hard to live that outside, in a society that takes and takes, a society that changes, rearranges, interprets and interprets some more, until there's nothing left but confusion. There isn't any sense ... any real sense of preservation or of keeping anything intact, not even what is sacred. Sure, we have traditional copyrights on songs, stories composed by people, and there's a different kind of copyright on the songs and stories that are sacred, it's all oral and those copyrights are respected, and no one would dream of breaking that. But when outsiders come in and are included in the sharing of these things, they think it's alright to claim them because no one said, 'You can't,' or because there's no contract. But the very sharing of those things is a contract, and there has to be respect for the sharing.

But in *Jessica*, who created the story? I didn't create it myself and you didn't either. We have to stop thinking 'you and me.' There were other people in the room whose energy, yes, even words, went into creating it, and here we are spreading our wings and saying, 'Mine.' That's what people do with lands when they fight over them....

LINDA But on the white side of the homestead, somebody might live on a piece of land, and not be able to make a go of it, and leave. Somebody else comes in and the winter gets them. Maybe they leave a shack, or one field cleared. Somebody else comes in, and somehow, that family clears the land, breaks the rocks, makes

enough room for a garden, waters the plants, looks up
at the sky – will there will be rain, will there be
drought, will there be snow? Too much, too little?
Then when the first crop comes in, you feel that you,
with the earth, and you, with your will, and you, with
your prayer have created something, so you can live
on that land. I've worked on *Jessica* until I thought I'd
go crazy – nine, ten complete drafts. I'm still working
on it. I've cared for it as I've never cared for anything
in my life. I stand on the land that is *Jessica* because I'm
the mother that tilled that soil. That's where I come
from too, and I don't think it's entirely reprehensible,
although I know it completely wrecked the land for
your people.

MARIA That's right.

LINDA The nerve we keep hitting that's so raw, maybe it
always will be raw. It's like a lover leaving you, they
walk in the room and you still feel it. What I loved
about what you told me, was that it was a journey of a
life, a huge bite of a life. It wasn't good and it wasn't
bad, it encompassed a whole sweep of human
experience. I felt like nothing beside that ... like Jessica.

Believing

MARIA If I started to think about it, 'Do I believe in them or
don't I?,' then I probably wouldn't believe in them, so
I don't try to analyze. When I'm feeling doubtful, I
look outside, and I know bloody well I couldn't make
a tree, or make the grass grow, or make the thunder
roll. Believing in it has nothing to do with it, it's just
there, and unless somebody can come up with a better
answer, the Creator, the mother, the father, the
grandfathers and the grandmothers, those make sense
to me, and an old man with a beard watching me,
judging me, doesn't make sense. I don't know about
the hodgepodge of things that are happening today.
All of a sudden there are witches and palm readers
and goodness knows what. I feel about them the way I
feel about some Native people who say they are elders

and teachers. If I don't like the feel of them, I stay
away. I don't want to sit around wasting my time
worrying about whether I believe or don't believe. I
know I have a family and a community. I know the
thunder rolls, the rain falls, and then there are my
friends. It doesn't sound all that powerful, spiritual
and magical, but it's real, that's it.

LINDA But you still pray, and speak of the grandmothers and
the spirits.

MARIA Of course I do, because they're real too. Real's got
nothing to do with believing or not believing.

Theatre Passe Muraille

LINDA It's very nice for me to be interested in Indian
mythology and these spiritual things. It's very nice.
It's a whole other thing to write about that world as if
it existed. When I was directing *Jessica* in Toronto,
there was this great guy who auditioned for
Wolverine. We needed someone who could double as
the lawyer and Wolverine. It was a hell of a
combination, because the actors who could play a
good straight lawyer couldn't get anywhere near
Wolverine, and vice versa. So this actor comes in, and
he's been working at the Stratford Festival or the
Shaw Festival for about fifteen years, and Passe
Muraille was almost at its weirdest and poorest then.
There was no money at the theatre. We just opened up
the doors and people seemed to arrive to rehearse all
kinds of things at all hours of the day and night. One
girl was living at the theatre, I think she was directing
a play, doing some office work and sleeping in this
corner near the Backspace. The place was filthy, with
mice, cockroaches, piles of old sets and backdrops all
over. It was great. I mean, this is what I loved about it.
I mean, it was an insane place. People coming and
going, rehearsing in corners. Because when there's no
money, you can at least offer the space.

So this classical actor comes in, and it's like he's
never seen the inside of this kind of theatre. He comes

in, looking around. He's read the play, and he turns to me and says, 'This is very interesting, but are you ... are you saying that it's *true*?' He was the only person – not a critic, nobody – who actually asked that question. Not 'a facinating blend of realities,' or 'Jungian archetypes reexamined,' but, 'What are you actually saying beyond that?' Then the actor looks around, and he sees the girl, who's just making her bed, and he says, 'Does she live here?' And I say, 'Yes.' He says, 'I'm just dying to work at a theatre like this.'

Community Canada

LINDA My community is this stubborn, wishy-washy, sentimental ghost-like people. Canadians. You call yourself a community worker and I feel I know what that means. Well, what's my community? Do I feel responsible for the community here? I sort of do. I'm a part of it, I work consciously for the survival of my culture. But sometimes I feel like we're ghosts with this losing battle. On top of the Native genocide comes another genocide of this paler thing, that is a people who resisted the American revolution, resisted that kind of political upheaval, but also resisted the imperialism from England and are involved in this struggle to discover the mythology of their own land. I mean, we don't own our land either. For brief periods of time we've owned our land. But what land do we own now? The north is filled with submarines. The government of the Northwest Territories has just said, 'We've already been invaded.' This territory belongs to the multinationals, to the American military forces, and will continue to belong to them. Our water is going to be sold, our trees, our cultural stuff ... sold. You finally found your ground, and you stand on it. But I feel like a ghost. I go to stand on my ground and find out it's been sold. Where's my ancestral home? The suburban home in Montreal that's sold, and now the suburban home in Kingston that's exactly like it? Is my home this house that I just bought? Do I feel connected to Toronto? Does anybody? The lack of a sense of place makes you feel ghostly. Why do I still cling to the theatre? Because it's the only ground I feel I have.

MARIA I don't understand Canadians.

LINDA Canadians don't understand Canadians.

MARIA I have these really strong feelings about them, but I can't ever say anything, because nobody ever tells me what in the hell, or who in the hell, they are.

LINDA It's not a tradition. It's bits and pieces. We're entirely immigrants. We all come from somewhere else. People trace their families back to a boat....

MARIA Well, if you guys came on a boat from Scotland, then Scotland is your ... home. Why would it be so hard?

LINDA Canadians know all kinds of stories about their ancestors. They trace family trees. They know what county they came from in England. But ask them about their own bloody grandfather that lived right here and it's, 'He was born, he lived and he died.'

MARIA Are you ashamed of them?

LINDA No. We're ashamed of not being powerful.

MARIA Americans accepted that they were a conquered people, and they became conquerors. But when they came, they knew they were a conquered people. Somehow, Canadians don't think that they were ever conquered. I've run into people who say, 'My great grandfather came from a little town in Derry,' or 'So-and-so came from the Highlands.' But they don't allow themselves to talk about why their people came. You did not come here as conquerors. You came here broken down and conquered. And as long as you refuse to look at that history, of course you'll be ghosts, because you have no place to come from. Ghosts are in purgatory, they're someplace in between. You refuse to believe it was ever done to you. I mean, you talk about me having a treasure full of diamonds and precious stones that you want to do something with, a whole bunch of Canadians think that the only treasures they've got is what's here.

LINDA I think the big gap is in our history here, not there.

MARIA Well, I don't know. Using the word ghost is good because that's what the old people say when they talk about white people in this country: 'Ghosts trying to find their clothes.' And to me they're ghosts because I don't understand where they're coming from. I turned on the television the other day, and there was an Orange parade on. And there were thousands of people lined up, cheering and going on and on. What do those people know about the Orange Society and what that represents? Do they know it's history? Do they know how it affected many of them? I read that there was an Orange parade in Ireland a few years ago, and the band that led them was from Toronto. It was an honour, I guess. I wonder what would happen if my people were invited to go to Ireland by the IRA to lead a parade, would the press call that an 'honour'? We would be on a hit list. What do people know when they have those parades? When I go to a Round Dance, I know what I'm celebrating.

LINDA The Orange lodges here are just some old guys, sitting around drinking beer. It's watered down. It doesn't mean the same thing in the New World. That trip across the ocean, and the generations after, changed everything. The Orange parade is a part of *The Farm Show*. It's presented ironically, with a funny kind of love.

MARIA Watered down.... I know what the Orange Society represents. I know what it did in my community. For nearly a hundred years, every single scrap of anything our old people had, they had to hide. Our leaders were jailed, hanged. Your people think of it as something in the Old Country. It's part of my history and yours.... I can't understand how anyone can go to a ceremony and not know what it is.

LINDA But the problem is not what happened in the Old Country, but what happened here. There isn't a decent history book about the amazing and bizarre things that happened to whites when they arrived here. I know you never understood why I felt such a need to go into the Native stuff. It's because I was born here, not there. Paul's lesson was, 'Plant your feet on the ground and see what you feel, what images come.' And when we did that, we got to a certain point and did a show about it. Every time I've done it, I've felt myself go a little deeper. Well, it's very thin soil we have here, and underneath it is you guys.

MARIA Why not look at who drove you out of your land? If we're ever going to make change, like, you know, understand each other....

LINDA I know who did. The people, the mentality that drove my ancestors out of their land ... the same bloody family compact runs this country now. It feels like an unbroken line sometimes. I know I'm from the underneath because of the way I feel, because of the anger I feel. I feel like I'm shaking my fist at someone on top of me, and I look ... I'm from the Canadian middle classes, who the hell am I shaking my fist at? Myself? Who is it I'm so angry at, that I feel has oppressed me? All I know is that I'm there with my fist in the air, feeling like most modern people, angry at shadows and ghosts. You want to make it into a clean story about conquerors and oppression, but it's not as clean or clear a story as you seem to think. Not for me. You say that if we understood our history, everything would be stronger. But it doesn't feel like that to me. We have to see in what way we're being conquered right now.

I watch an aging pride when I go to gatherings in Toronto. There's a community of about a thousand people, the artists who stayed here instead of leaving, and all of them have fought a battle to break through every kind of snotty colonialism in order to free themselves to be fascinated by their own place. They haven't left their people, you would say, and they've paid for it because their own people often despise them for it. That's my community.

MARIA Your people think they're not oppressed. If you're not oppressed, then what in the world is everybody so uptight about? I think sometimes you guys are a hundred times more oppressed than we are.

Somebody's got you guys believing you've got the power, and there's nobody as poor as poor white people. How can you help them, when you refuse to recognize your history? Once you recognize that you were robbed, then you have a place to begin.

LINDA But that's the place where I did ... where I have begun.

MARIA Canadians didn't come in and slaughter us like the Americans did their Aboriginal people, they were nice guys, just forced us on our knees and said, 'We'll keep them there forever.' I mean, Canadians have either got to become good guys or they've got to become bad guys; otherwise, I guess it's purgatory forever.

LINDA Hear hear.

MARIA I know I'm of this country. I know I'm Metis. I'm of this land. Then I guess I'm a Canadian, because that's who the conqueror happens to be today. Who the fuck knows who it's going to be tomorrow?

The Process

MARIA It's easier to go and do it yourself, and face the conflict after ... the hard words and stuff, but not the actual pain of trying to do it together. The process has been really gruelling for both of us, and maybe white people don't want to go through that, maybe they would rather just do it themselves, because it's too much hassle dealing with two hundred years of bad times. But if people are to work together they've got to go through that process, or the trust won't happen – on a superficial level maybe, but not on a real level. Maybe no one has time, I don't know, Linda.... Maybe I'm just a real bitch like some people think, but I don't think so, no, I can't buy that.... God, what am I saying? My mistrust comes from our history, but I'll come halfway, because I have to.

There are times when you and I are sitting down together, talking ... not when we're having these talks, but just the rest of the time that we're living in the house together. And I'll be doing something and you'll be doing something, and I'll look over at you, and you're totally alien to me. There's a flash ... that you're so different. I don't know you. I'm not related to you. It scares me. And when I get that flash, it again puts me on guard. I think, 'Be careful.' And, again, the fear is you're going to do it yourself. And I say to myself, if that happens, it'll only confirm the flashes that I got: 'Well, I knew that was going to happen, but I'll be okay. I'll be okay because it's only confirmed what I already knew.'

But that's not really it, I guess what really frightens me is, if that happens, you're going to come back again. You'll always keep coming back, and each time you come back, I have to sit down with you, because I can't let you go, just like you can't let me go.

Healing

LINDA The hatred I found inside ... I think that's sort of the trapped Wolverine, or the unbalanced Wolverine ... the self-hatred was so enormous, and so was the belief that I should punish myself, you could call it a sacrifice. At one point we got right into the Catholic stuff, and this doctor said, 'Do you believe you're suffering for other people?' And I said, 'Yes.' He said, 'Do you believe you're Jesus Christ?' And I said, 'Yes.' And then I thought, 'Ohh God, no. I'm a lunatic.' But I had to say it.

MARIA With the old religions, or spiritual ways, you had your time to sacrifice. For Native people it was the Sun Dance and the fasting time. Once you did that, then you went on with the job of living, you're not supposed to suffer all the time. The Creator didn't put you on the earth just to suffer, that was why we were given all the other things in our being.... The most important thing is to live a good life, to have health and happiness. Our Creator gave us all kinds of other emotions – love, joy – beautiful things, a physical body, spirituality, all of these things to make our lives rich. We don't get put here on the earth just to suffer. And then there's Christ, who has to carry his Cross all the time, they never let him off, he suffers all the time; and they tell us that he has to suffer for us, that's what he was put on the earth for, so it makes people feel guilty when we're.... Seems to me the elders make more sense when they say that the Creator, the all-power, is loving and wants us to reach our full potential. How on earth can we do that if we're carrying Crosses and laying our uglies on everybody? We end up with racism, lies, not knowing who or what we are, where we come from. We end up with sore backs, like you, with anger, like me.

LINDA   But the other night, when you talked about sacrifice, what were you saying then?

MARIA   When I said I understood ... that, finally, Jesus made sense to me?

LINDA   Yes.

MARIA   Well, what I was saying is that the elders, my old teachers, helped me to unblock, to start looking at Christianity ... my studying ancient religions helped.... I had to, because there was so much anger, sometimes it's hard for me to believe I have so much. Christianity, Catholicism in particular, came along and stole from the old things. The things that were important, sacred to people, things that were the life-blood of people, they took those things. Not everything, just the real power things. One of the real power things is sacrifice, for example, your time to sacrifice. Christ sacrificed himself because he was a holy man. He was a pipe carrier, for lack of a better word. He did something when he sacrificed himself ... and I'm not looking at the way the Church tells us he sacrificed himself. He hung on that tree. The women took him to the caves and he was put there for so many days. Those were all sacred things, teachings and ways that were practised for centuries before him. That sacrifice was an old ceremony, taking him to the caves. That was an old ceremony, the hanging. It's no different than hanging from the Sun Dance Tree. He did all of the things that were part of the old religion. The women who came and helped him, there were only women that took him

there. He was up there for so many days and then he
rose again. Well, that's what happens when we go up
to fast, or when we sacrifice ourselves. We're told ...
when we fast ... that once we come out, when we go
into the sweat lodge, we come out and we no longer
belong to this world. We belong to the spirit world
and we go out and we make our sacrifice, nobody can
talk to us, nobody sees us. So, that's like going up to
the cave. You come back down, nobody sees you,
nobody talks to you until after you've gone into the
sweat lodge again. The Spirits bring you back, and
they give you back to the people, and you're reborn.
That's what Christ did. He came back out of the caves
and people saw him. He was reborn. And then,
according to Christianity, he rose and went to heaven.
But how do we know that Christ didn't remain on
earth until he died of old age?

LINDA The New Testament is very careful about making sure
that we do believe.

MARIA I can look at my grandmother's old way, and it makes
sense, but the Christian way doesn't. Why? Because
the people who follow that way still make those kinds
of sacrifices, and they respect themselves and other
peoples. They don't try to change other people or tell
them they are wrong. If the Christian way is right,
why are they so miserable, and why is it so important
to them to rip away and ridicule the sacred things of
other people? But what happened with the Christians
is they don't practise the teachings of their holy man,
instead it's okay to hurt other people because 'I'll pray
on Sunday, and the man who carries the Cross for us
will look after it.' The old way says we are all
responsible for Creation and for each other.

LINDA Like, the power is within us.

MARIA We never feel the power's within us, with the
Christian way. We never feel the incredible feeling of
going to the spirit world, and coming back out, and
the closeness to all things that gives us. Suffering has a
flip side, it has the joy of coming through the pain, the
joy that you've done it, you've been able to make the

ultimate sacrifice. Religion makes us carry it around all day long until we ... we mess up our families, we mess up our kids, we mess up our grandchildren, we abuse our kids and they become abusers for ten generations after. And we abuse everything around us, because we have no power inside of us. When we make our own sacrifice, we are cleansed when it is finished. You've done it. You've walked through it. You've been able to do it. You've been able to touch the Creation. You've been able to touch the mother, the father. You've felt all of them, and you've come out, and your eyes are bright and clear and you feel dreamy. You feel at one with everything. You feel like your sister is really your sister, you feel like your dad is really your dad. You make these connections, and they're healthy and clean and joyful.

LINDA   Oh, we're a couple of Catholics. I mean, what can we say? A couple of Catholics!

MARIA   I'm not a Catholic.

LINDA   No, of course not.

MARIA   The things that they took are sacred things that belong to all of our old people, all over the earth. Reminds me of this poem I wrote one time, that just came out of nowhere....

Who are you, stalking the fringes of our circles,
singing your songs of doom.
You sing of grandfather, grandmother, love,
but your voice is accompanied by the music of
inquisitions.

It doesn't matter what colour you are, there is always some religion that stalks around trying to take all the things away from people. I mean, where is it getting us? Holes in the ozone layer, winds nobody can control, heat nobody can control, floods, all kinds of stuff. The earth is hurting so bad, and they're still stealing. They're still stealing to make bigger things, to make bigger holes, to do bigger things. They're frightening. That's why we've got to get strong. That's why we've got to understand that we have to make

those connections. We're writers, we're artists, we
have to give people back their stuff. People are going
to laugh at us. They're going to think we're a couple of
kooks. But there are other people out there doing the
same thing we are. There are singers that are doing it,
and writers that are doing it ... dancers ... and we're
doing it. Those are the prophecies. Or else we're just
going to go crazy one day. Or she's going to say,
'Enough. That's enough.' And this place is just going
to be devastated. There have to be healers and
teachers. We have to remember that we can't ever do
it their way again, we have to be balanced. This all
makes us sound like we're going to be a couple of
evangelists....

But I feel like, Linda, I feel ... I can feel it every
single day. I feel it in the city. It's like I can hear little
bits of songs here and there. And you can hear that
pain all over. You can feel that pain all over from
people, and that fear. It's coming really fast.

LINDA People say, 'It's hot,' and there's real fear in their eyes.
In my eyes. What if it's hotter next year, and hotter the
next year?

MARIA But the doom and the stuff that they feel, and the fear
in their eyes, that's our job. I mean, we don't go out
and carry placards. It's stuff like this. We have to talk
to the people that are going to read these pages.
They'll understand. They'll know what we're talking
about. They will. They understood what *Jessica* was
about. They went away crying. They understood.
They understand. When we listen to somebody sing a
song, we understand. Every single little time that
somebody reads a word in here that makes them feel
good, it means we made them a little bit stronger ...
and we make ourselves a little bit stronger.

The Contract

MARIA There's something we're still not talking about ... the
stuff about the contract.

LINDA I know....

MARIA   It's right there in the middle of the whole thing ... if I was reading this, I'd say, 'There's something there that they're not telling.'

LINDA   It's because he's not here to speak for himself....

MARIA   So we just skirt around him, like a lie in the middle. For me, it's important because he's the reason why I reacted the way I did. I maybe would have been mad at you anyway, but not like that, not two years' worth.

LINDA   I didn't know what was....

MARIA   He's responsible for a lot of what happened ... and he comes out pretty good in this.

LINDA   I know, I've made sure that he did ... he's suffered in his own way.

MARIA   But look at us, we're protecting him when he's the reason we didn't speak for so long. You want to talk about the matriarchies giving up the power, but I don't believe it. Men came in the way they always do, and caused the problem, and left the women at each other's throats. Then they took it. Look what happened to us. I'm not supposed to tell the story because it will hurt him? He came in between, the conqueror with his piece of paper, when we were both exhausted and wrecked. It's taken us all this time to work it out, because I've still got that inside.

LINDA   I feel like I've been paying for that contract thing forever with you....

MARIA   It's that smiling Virgin Mary again, being nice, taking it and taking it, and smoothing it over so men will look good. They painted that smile on her face so she wouldn't open her mouth. Never getting angry and saying, 'No.' I could have given up, just said, 'I'll sign the damn thing,' but I didn't.

LINDA   It's true.

MARIA   I kept saying, let's get a contract, let's do it now, because I don't like working without one. Then he just put it in front of me at a coffee shop and said, 'Sign it.' When I looked at it, it had the theatre owning film rights, video rights, television rights....

LINDA   I did look at it, I'm not entirely innocent, but I didn't understand what any of it meant ... that's true. I left all that kind of stuff up to 'male energy.' Well, maybe if I'd given it importance, the big break between us wouldn't have happened. I knew 25th Street House was in a crisis about money then – what theatre isn't always in a crisis about money – and that they were trying to figure out how to make money back on the new plays that were good, to pay for the disasters.

MARIA   But I would have understood that ... I wouldn't have given everything away, but if it had been explained to me we could have worked something out.... Paul confirmed all my fears, and worse.

    I don't remember how long after the play opened that I met Paul in that coffee shop. I think he was leaving in the afternoon for Toronto, and I was really looking forward to sitting down and talking with him about 'the process.' I thought 'This is my chance, now he'll talk to me.' And he gave me that contract and asked me to sign it. I started to read the contract, and he said we'd already talked about it before, and we had, over the course of the rehearsals and stuff, but we never really got down to it. I read it and the contract said that you would have first refusal rights on who would play Jessica. But you and I had already said that after this time Jessica would have to be played by a Native woman. And I know what 'first refusal' means with a publisher, that means you can't go to anyone else, so if you decided to do it, you could do it forever after. I wanted to direct Jessica next, and I wanted to do it with a Native woman. That was something I thought you understood, because we'd talked about it and you'd agreed. Another clause in the contract was the video and screenplay rights, and I don't remember how that was broken down, but all of a sudden I would have to share with 25th Street House Theatre, with you, and with Paul. I understood sharing with you and Paul, but nobody had ever said anything about the Theatre owning anything. And that really made me angry, because two film producers had flown in for opening night and negotiations were already beginning for a film, and

the negotiations were for *Halfbreed* and also the stuff
in *Jessica*. I questioned those clauses, and Paul refused
to discuss them. All he said was that a theatre always
owns part of a play, and I knew that to be untrue. All
of the stuff through the play came to a head, and I just
exploded. I refused to sign, and Paul said, 'Well, it's
two against one.'

All I remember is knocking everything off the table,
I remember the salt shaker falling off the table. I
remember the name of the place, 'Johnny's Cafe,'
because whenever I have to negotiate something now,
I go there and have a cup of coffee.

The ugliest part of the contract was that I had never
been consulted, and it reminded me of the treaties,
being asked to put my 'X' on something, and I didn't
even get the right of an interpreter. My great-great-
grandfather was head chief and signed Treaty Six. But
he was there to negotiate, and he had an interpreter,
and this was nineteen eighty-whatever, and I wasn't
given any respect at all. It's like when we talk about
whether the matriarchies gave it away.... I don't
believe they did, no matter how you try to cover up
for the patriarchy, I don't believe they ever gave it
away. I think what happened is that an emissary came,
just like the fur traders and the missionaries came to
the Indian people, like Paul came with you, and over a
period of time they worked on the good faith of the
people, established trust, and then they took it. So all
these years, there's always been the mistrust, there's
always been a wall, no matter how I tried to get close
to you, to understand you.... You'd be really open with
me, and I'd see this wall come up, and I would think
about what Paul did, and I'd think you were going to
do the same thing. Always I felt you were lying to me.
I've never been able to understand why. I always
thought you knew about the contract, that you were
part of writing it up, and whenever I mentioned it,
you'd sort of go blank, and say you didn't know
anything about it. And I feel like I can't ever really say
what I have to say, because what I have to say is not to

you, it's to Paul. Maybe that's why I have such a thing about the Orange Society now. For years I used to tease Paul, saying, 'Just imagine what Gabriel would say if he knew I was working with an Orangeman.' And even now, I'm getting this off my chest but I still feel like ... here's you and me, we've agonized through this whole thing, but what we've both been doing is protecting Paul. He hasn't had to suffer through your bad back like I've had to, he hasn't had to go through my rages like you've had to. Because whenever you talk about Pan being the god of theatre, every time you and I are together, I see Paul sitting back against a bunch of cushions, pulling his beard, always watching us to see how we'll behave next, what we'll do next. I feel like grabbing him by the hair and throwing him out on the stage, and saying, 'Okay man, speak.'

Paul

VOICE FROM THE MIDDLE OF THE ROOM That's not going to work. I've said it before – my place is not on stage.

MARIA AND LINDA What do you mean?

VOICE FROM THE MIDDLE OF THE ROOM Look. We tried that once. I went on stage with the actors. They booted me off the stage, made me promise never to go back, and they were right. My place is here. Sitting in the middle of the room. Making suggestions, hoping, willing it to happen, but not doing it. There is certainly no place here for my story.

MARIA AND LINDA Hold on, you're not going to get off that easily.

VOICE FROM THE MIDDLE OF THE ROOM Look, you have been going on for over a hundred pages and you still haven't mentioned my favourite memories: the night Graham and I whistled down the northern lights in Edmonton, the time Maria ordered me to take James Joyce out for a drink of whisky and a cigarette (neither of which I can personally stand), and finally, the sweat lodge held at Duck Lake by Junior and his helper with the unbelievable name of Brutus. None of these are included and it's quite right that they aren't. For it's become clear to me that the progress of this play has grown closer and closer to the lives of Linda and Maria, and so for me, as for Alice at the tea party, the facts cry out, 'No room, no room!' I don't fit. But I will offer a few observations.

This method of making plays is a complicated and, as we can see from the above, an often painful experience. All shows hurt to do. The concentration required, the personal energy and the need to go outside of oneself and meet these other experiences are not for the fragile. The one reassuring fact, if indeed there can be any reassurance, is that everybody 'hurts' doing them, including the guy sitting in the middle of the room. Often when the play goes on stage and is successful, the difficulties of rehearsal are forgotten or romanticized; but when I look back on a whole list of original works, I see the same moments of doubt, the same stone walls where the ideas stopped, and the same sense that we would never get the story right. I think I used to apologize for this part of the work method, but in more recent times I just shrug, and like Miller's Willy Loman, have recognized that 'it goes with the territory.'

There is one additional painful process that is reserved for the director. Maria, I tried to explain it to you the night after the opening of *Jessica* in Saskatoon. Usually, after opening night, my energy has been used up and I fall into a depression. I feel of no further use to the show. The actors have taken over their characters, and the audience is about to take over the play. No role for me. So I have had to find some means of giving the play away. Actually, it's more a matter of making myself realize that the play no longer requires my watching it. It's taken a flight of its own. So we attended a performance of a touring French show and I tried to explain how the play was no longer there. I guess I wasn't very clear, but then, personal psychology is not my strong suit. The strength for me lies in the play and the power of the play when it gets picked up by an audience. As such, the performances of *Jessica* in Saskatoon were exceptional personal and public statements. They were also a major advance for the inclusion of real magic in our theatre, and they were a popular success.

In the past, such success gave signs as to where the production of the play should then head. In this case, it didn't. I don't know why. Perhaps it was the confusing tenor of the times (there was a real economic crisis in '82), or perhaps it was because of the volatile nature of the material in the show. Anyway, I was at a standstill. We had a hit, and I had no idea what to do with it.

I guess this is where the contract comes in. From my point of view, the actual contract is what Linda called it – a red herring. It was invented by a long-departed, over-zealous new administrator at 25th Street House Theatre to protect that theatre from 'eastern sharpies.' The Theatre had been very generous in its support of the play and this was their pound of flesh. In my opinion, from a legal point of view the contract wasn't worth the paper it was written on. Maybe the same is true for Treaty Six. However, it was an explosive issue and sent all three of our relationships spinning. I suspect if it hadn't been this problem, another would have been found. It is true that questions of ownership and responsibility in such a collaboration are very touchy points and difficult to define. This is obviously more so when you are collaborating on a real person's life story. It was probably inevitable that since we had put so much hope and energy into the show, no mere mortal success could satisfy us.

There is an ironic point in all of this – perhaps easier to see if you are the guy sitting in the middle of the room. All of the frustration and the potential for mistrust fueled the future work on the play, underscoring its themes of racial tension, as well as emphasizing the problems of male-female relations. It also propelled Maria and Linda into the transconti-nental dance of understanding/misunderstanding which is at the core of their chronicle. The final version of *Jessica* is the richer for all of our experiences and the story of Linda's and Maria's journey has become a fabulous tale of its own. In fact, it would make an interesting play. If anyone is interested in working on that venture, I'm still sitting in the middle of the room, and available. The process works.

The Red Cloth

MARIA   I remember when I was a little girl, and we were going to a Sun Dance, and there was a 'give-away' after. My grandmother had the big blanket spread on the floor the night before, and all of us had to put things in there, for the give-away. The day before she had given me some cloth for a dress. It was very special, it was a print, but it was the colour I wanted, red. I knew my grandmother knew how much that cloth meant to me, but I thought I could fool her. You see, your most prized possession should be what goes to the give-away.

So I made a big deal about looking through my stuff, you know – 'No, I don't think I'll give that' – trying to fool her into believing that something else was more important than the cloth. I did this whole act, looking at my favourite hair combs, looking at the cloth, deciding to give the cloth away, as if it meant nothing; then, as if the hair combs meant more, taking the cloth out and putting the combs in. I did that with almost everything I had, the cloth went in and out several times, then finally I took the cloth out of there and I said, 'No.'

My grandmother never said anything, she was just sitting there looking at me while she smoked. She knew what I was doing and I was ashamed. I put the cloth on the blanket and I started to cry. I knew I wouldn't have a new dress. My grandmother waited until I finished crying and said, 'The give-away should hurt, that's your sacrifice.'

I went to that Sun Dance, and the whole time it was on, I saw that cloth. My focus, which was supposed to be on praying and sacrificing, was on that cloth. I thought about it for the whole four days we were there, and when the give-away came, I stared at the lady that was given that cloth. And I thought, 'What did you do to deserve it? It's not yours.'

And you know, for years after, even today, when I go back to that community, and I see that woman, who's now an old lady, I always remember, 'This is the lady who got the cloth, this is who got that bloody cloth.' Isn't that awful? Because she's always so happy to see me. She hasn't a clue.

I have a memory like an elephant when something is special to me. I'm not like that about everything, I give lots of stuff away, but every once in a while.... And I have to work on that almost everyday.... I'm really quite stingy ... God, I hate to admit that. Whenever I really love something, I can see my granny watching me.

LINDA The clearest give-away I have ever been involved in has been *Jessica*. It has that feeling to it. It's my red cloth. And yet, I wouldn't have not done it for the world.

Peace

MARIA The anger is gone, but I need to feel like everything's okay between the two of us. And I was kind of dreading that.

LINDA Yeah.

MARIA There's just this mangled stuff all over the place, but it's not hurting anymore.... In fact, when I think about it now, it was one hell of an experience.

LINDA Yeah.

MARIA Something is gone. I know that you're not going to get all wrecked again. You're going to be okay, and so I feel okay. You know? And whatever thing it was that I thought was gone inside of me, the last little piece is now back in place. I'm tired, and I would just like to pack up and go home next week, as fast as I can. I want to finish this. I'm excited about it, but for the first

time I'm excited about going home, because I know
I'm not going with this damn thing sitting on my back.

LINDA But ... you will ... I mean ... there's the editing and
the....

MARIA Going home and doing work is one thing, but I don't
have all that other stuff to take back with me anymore.
It's like, whatever it is, 'There she is now.' We're
outside of it. It can't hurt us anymore.

LINDA I think we'd better quit. Let's have a glass of wine.

Peace?

LINDA I've been reading it over Maria, and.... Are we going to
leave people with the faerie tale of it? Because the
truth is, I am wrecked over doing this, I'm still afraid
of you, still feel like your servant. I'm still hurt and
angry about so many things....

MARIA I know, I was thinking about that too. I get these
flashes of anger sometimes, and I know you do too.
Maybe I should put in that letter I wrote....

LINDA No, not the letter, please, not the letter....

MARIA It's as if you're trying to get me angry and uptight
again....

LINDA No, I just want to say everything, so you don't have a
chance to get mad when it's done. I'm not into
pussyfooting around anymore.

MARIA You see? When you admit you're a thief, then you can
be honourable.

LINDA Is that all you can think of still? Is this whole thing a
lie?

MARIA It's not a lie, it's just a wound we want to be healed
sooner than is possible. Maybe it'll take a hundred
years. Angry or not, I feel good, and that's a lot better
than feeling angry and bad.

LINDA I wander around, working on this, just raging away at
you, but I truly love you Maria.

MARIA I don't know if I'll ever stop being angry with you, but
I want to adopt you [*laughing*], so I can get after you
the same way I get after my own daughters.... What
am I saying? I must be out of my mind.

Jessica

Characters

JESSICA   Metis. Female. Stubborn, feisty, a survivor. Has the qualities of all her spirits and more. A complex woman struggling to come into her power.

COYOTE   Fast, the ultimate adaptor. Has a swishy tail and a swishy logic. Coyote transforms to: VITALINE, Jesse's spiritual teacher. An old Native woman, or so it appears. Her mind goes in circles and don't you forget it.

BEAR   Warm. Sensual. Powerful. Loving, but don't cross him. Bear tranforms to: SAM, a Native activist. Jesse's lover. A warrior searching for the honourable fight.

UNICORN   One-horned beast from the old power. Wild. Sexual. Fluid. She's been hiding out since the days of the goddess. Unicorn transforms to: LIZ, white blonde callgirl. Jesse's friend. She's seen a lot, most of it bad.

WOLVERINE   Will tear an animal three times its size to pieces. Dark. Vicious. Bloody. Desires revenge. Wolverine transforms to: BOB, a white lawyer on his way to the top. Until he meets Jessica. Not an unattractive man.

CROW   Jesse's childhood spirit and special guardian. Unreliable, furry, defensive, inventive. He plays many roles, but always remains Crow. Just a gambler at heart. He bets on Jessica.

Notes

Jessica was first co-produced by 25th Street House Theatre in Saskatoon, and Theatre Passe Muraille in Toronto, in October 1981. The cast was:

JESSICA Linda Griffiths
COYOTE Tantoo Cardinal
CROW Tom Hauff
BEAR Graham Greene

Written by: Maria Campbell, Linda Griffiths,
    Paul Thompson.
Directed by: Paul Thompson.
Set and costume: Don Rutley.
Masks: Heather Larson.

The rewritten *Jessica* was produced by Theatre Passe Muraille in Toronto, February, 1986, with the following cast:

JESSICA Monique Mohica
COYOTE / VITALINE Makka Kliest
BEAR / SAM Gary Farmer
CROW Tom Jackson
WOLVERINE / BOB Victor Ertmanis
UNICORN / LIZ Susan Hogan

Written by: Linda Griffiths,
    in collaboration with Maria Campbell.
Directed by: Linda Griffiths and Clarke Rogers.
Stage Manager: Sandi Cumberland.
Set by: Marilyn Berkovich.
Masks by: Jerrard Smith.
Lights by: Steve Allan with Jim Plaxton.
Costumes by: Paul Kelman.
Original Music: David Akal Jaggs.
Pre-production: Christopher Gerrard Pinker.

Subsequently, in the fall of 1986, Theatre Passe Muraille remounted *Jessica* to play at the Great Canadian Theatre Company in Ottawa, and the Toronto Free Theatre in Toronto. The cast was:

JESSICA	Tantoo Cardinal
COYOTE / VITALINE	Makka Kliest
CROW	Graham Greene
BEAR / SAM	Tom Jackson
WOLVERINE / BOB	David Conor (Ottawa)
	and
	Peter MacNiel (Toronto)

Written by: Linda Griffiths,
   in collaboration with Maria Campbell.
Directed by: Clarke Rogers.
Stage Manager: Joa Boacha.
Masks by: Jerrard Smith.
Touring Set: Jim Plaxton, based on
   original design by Marilyn Berkovich.
Lights: Steve Allan.
Original Music: David Akal Jaggs.

Act One

In the darkness we hear night noises. The sound of wind,
wings; something scuttles, almost laughs, an owl calls.
    As if on the periphery of vision, we see the briefest flash
of a coal black feather, catch the reflection of an unseen
movement, almost glimpse a white shadow in a corner.
    Revealed by the growing light is an old Native woman,
VITALINE, *sitting in her cabin. Her presence is electric, her*
energy a lightning rod, yet she appears calm, still. As the
sounds build around her, she gathers power, throws back her
head, and screams.

A flash.
Vitaline transforms to Coyote.
Masked Spirits appear.
They are humorous, sensual, deadly.

BEAR She's doing something....

WOLVERINE She wants something....

COYOTE She's going fast, could be too fast....

BEAR Maybe not, Coyote, maybe not....

COYOTE You're right, maybe it's too slow....

BEAR She's one of the last ones who knows how to surprise us.

COYOTE I was dancing, around and through the crowd, they were cheering me, they couldn't believe how I moved....

WOLVERINE I'd been stalking him for weeks, he was almost mad. His mouth was open, howling, and now this.

BEAR She could still be dreaming....

COYOTE She dreams us or we dream her, what's the difference?

BEAR It's been a long time since one of them has taken power for themselves....

COYOTE Maybe she doesn't know what she's doing....

BEAR She knows alright, she's challenging us....

WOLVERINE Why?

BEAR   We'll wait. Where is the Crow?

COYOTE   In a bar, where else?

WOLVERINE   This is a waste of time.

[CROW *dashes in, dishevelled, carrying a pool cue*]

CROW   Ripped away, there's no other word for it. There I was in the bar, buying rounds all night, then just when it was my turn – wham! White lightning.

BEAR   Vitaline went right through the roof when she called us....

CROW   It's those dreams, I knew the Wolverine was going too far....

Tangled harp strings.
Smoke.
Unicorn wakes.
Her back arches,
she leaps to her feet.

WOLVERINE   What is too far, Crow?

COYOTE   [*seeing the* UNICORN] Look!

CROW   This might be too far. It's dangerous.

COYOTE   You're going to be sorry if you don't look.

BEAR   Vitaline knows the danger, she's asking us to wait.

COYOTE   Just ... forget it.

CROW   But what's it about?

BEAR   Jessica.

CROW   I should have known. [CROW *finally sees the* UNICORN] Look!

[*The* SPIRITS *watch in amazement as the* UNICORN *makes her way toward them. She turns in a circle and stops*]

CROW   What is that?

BEAR   Widdershins.

UNICORN   What's wild deserves to live, that's all I can say.

CROW   What?

UNICORN   What's wild deserves to live, otherwise we're all fucked.

COYOTE   I think I like her, but then again, I think I don't.

CROW   Vitaline must've called her up, but from where?

BEAR   I'm starting to remember....

UNICORN   I was stuck. I just couldn't get over the glory days. There was wildness. And lunacy. And ecstasy. I was magic, birth was magic, sex was magic, shit was magic, dancing, singing, fucking ... maybe it went too far.... Then it was too late ... so tired ... am I in the wrong place again? You're part of the old way, aren't you?

CROW I'm Native to this place, let's put it that way.

UNICORN I'm talking about the old days, the real old days, when a horn in your forehead really meant something.

BEAR [*remembering something from the distant past*] OOOoooooooohhhhh, the Grandmothers! She's come so far....

COYOTE [*to* UNICORN] I saw you at the Bay, you had a big pink bow and you were sitting on a candy cane rainbow.

UNICORN Innana Morigana Dana Huldah Mahh!

COYOTE I think she's swearing. She's inside out, just like Jessica.

UNICORN Jessica.

[JESSICA *runs onto the stage, desperate, as if being chased. She stops suddenly, hearing something*]

CROW That's not my fault.

COYOTE You were her first spirit, Crow, Jesse's got too many feathers and not enough tail.

CROW You could say she's had too much tail and not enough beak.

COYOTE Ha!

Jessica starts,
causing
a whine of static.
Coyote transforms to Vitaline.

[VITALINE *begins puttering in the kitchen.* JESSICA *enters the cabin, her insides shredded like raw meat*]

VITALINE I knew you were coming back, I put on some of that tea you're always drinking, that camelhump stuff.

JESSICA I don't want any tea, Vitaline.

VITALINE Good, then you're finally ready to drink some of my coffee, I know I put it somewhere....

JESSICA No coffee.

VITALINE You look like some old dog that hasn't had a scratch in years....

JESSICA I can't do it. I'm going away.

VITALINE Some old dog slinking down some back road, with me coming after her with a stick in my hand....

JESSICA I'm the one with the stick. He was down on the floor, I was on top of him with my hands around his throat....

VITALINE Did you kill him?

JESSICA I don't remember ... no.

VITALINE No big problem then.

JESSICA What do you say when you take your claws away? Sorry about that, but I'm studying the old ways and my teacher says I have to go to the dark side, so please try to understand?

VITALINE This was that lawyer? He probably had it coming.

JESSICA It's over. I have to stop.

VITALINE You've got to stop, alright. Stop all that crazy talk before the spirits give you a good whack. I'm your teacher, I'm very smart, I've taught all kinds of people, one white guy even. I helped you find your power and you're saying I'm just some old woman raving away in the bush? Running around with eagle feathers sticking out of my head? That's what I am?

JESSICA No.

VITALINE What's the matter with you? Yes, you had to go to your dark side. You want to feel and understand your power?

JESSICA I don't know....

VITALINE You don't get a choice, you have to.

JESSICA You mean I can't go back.

VITALINE I mean you were strong and you were ready. Now you come here like some city animal, all drained out from that ... that....

JESSICA Electricity.

VITALINE I'll show you electricity.

Electric wail.
Vitaline becomes Coyote.
The Spirits zap into full action.
Coyote crashes into Unicorn,
gives a yelp,
transforms back to Vitaline.

[*Once more in her kitchen,* VITALINE *stares at the* COYOTE *mask in her hands. She finally senses the* UNICORN]

JESSICA [*not impressed*] You don't have to use tricks to show you can call Coyote, you're as tricky as she is, but it's still tricks.

VITALINE Something happened, I don't know what I did, but grandmother Coyote knows, that's for sure.

JESSICA I can't do it anymore. I'm not Indian, I'm not white, I'm a Halfbreed. I live in a white world full of filing cabinets and common sense. The years go by and everyone around me is making decisions and calming down, and my life just gets weirder ... no, it's worse than that ... waves and waves and waves of fear, I'm drowning and I'm cracking apart.

VITALINE Then you ask the spirits for help.

JESSICA It's gone, I can't pray, I can't feel them.... I've been faking it, you've been faking it, look at the real world....

[VITALINE *whacks* JESSICA *across the face*]

VITALINE You know more than I did when I was your age, but I wasn't so stubborn. Maybe I'm a bit jealous, I don't know.

JESSICA There is no song and no vision.

VITALINE And I know there is.... Maybe there's something in that life you live.... in those briefcases and papers, something I don't know about.... [*mumbling in Cree*] tapway aoko atikquay animina....

JESSICA I want to show you something. [*she opens her suitcase, pulling things from the mess inside*] We go to ceremonies, I have to change into a skirt ... I say, 'Why can't women wear pants?' Everyone looks at me like I'm crazy.... You see these jeans? They're a part of me. I sit in a room full of sweet grass and animal skins, with rattles and drums, as if I wasn't carrying a walkman and a computer the size of a briefcase. As if it was two hundred years ago. Vitaline, I like spike heels. I read Karl Marx and *People* magazine.

VITALINE There's plenty of white in you, lots of those stubborn Scottish people.... Okay, so that's your bundle.

JESSICA   It's not a bundle of anything, it's a suitcase.

VITALINE   [*thinking fast, the spirits won't wait forever*] If I say it's a bundle, then it is a bundle.... Okay, maybe we do a different kind of ceremony, maybe the things I've been doing aren't right for you. Bring me a package of smokes, not the sage....

    [*The* SPIRITS *react*]

    Yes, bring the sage, I better not get that brave.

JESSICA   What are you up to?

VITALINE   Do what I tell you. I'm going way out for you, my girl. Goodness knows what's going to happen to me this time. Set up this stuff like for a ceremony, put those shoes in the four corners, use those scarves too....

JESSICA   You can't do a ceremony....

    [VITALINE *is rumaging through the suitcase*]

    There's no pipe....

VITALINE   Put this on [*a scarf*], try putting on this bathrobe....

    [JESSICA *obeys*]

JESSICA   There's no nothing....

VITALINE   Put the papers in the middle ... [*gives her the walkman earphones*] get these in your ears.

JESSICA   [*obeys*] It won't work, it's not even dark.

VITALINE   It doesn't have to be dark.

JESSICA   We've always done everything according to tradition.

VITALINE   Isn't that what you're complaining about? [VITALINE *places the objects as if they were ceremonial*] If you respect those ways you can change them, if not, then you are faking it. Hurry. They're close, and they're waiting.

The Spirits gather uneasily.
Vitaline takes the sage,
centering her power, turns slowly
north, south, east, west.

VITALINE   My Creator. Spirits of the sea and air. Thunder beings. You who see in the dark. Grandmothers and Grandfathers, you who have protected us and guided us since we first took breath, hear me. Have pity on me, have pity on this woman. She has been learning the ways of power, learning in her own world, not always with my blessing, and now she is caught somewhere, between the light and darkness of her own spirit. I am afraid for her. I'm calling you with all my strength, but in a new way. You see my medicine lodge is very different today. This woman is of mixed blood, so this ceremony is of mixed blood. The city is with us, the white world is with us, there is a new energy that speaks to us. Our lodges changed with the coming of the horse and the coming of the white man....

BEAR   More with the coming of the horse than with the white man....

CROW   The horse was a better deal.

VITALINE   I ask you to let this woman enter the circle in her own way. I humbly ask you to help her.

WOLVERINE   [*refusing all change*] Haugghhhaughhhsstttttttttahhhgh!

BEAR   Vitaline, we're listening, but we're wondering what's going on. Anyone can call us, but to have a ceremony with no objects of power....

VITALINE   [*waves one of* JESSICA's *shoes*] These have power, Grandfather, believe me....

UNICORN   I like that, about the high heels.

BEAR   Vitaline, you know it's dangerous to mix up different kinds of power....

VITALINE   I'm mixing them up because they're mixed up in her life. I know that to challenge the lines of power is dangerous for all of us. But I feel something new from you,
[UNICORN *moves closer*]
something has happened, let it be for the good. Let Jessica speak now.

CROW   But what about this stuffed animal from Zellers? What do we do with her? Vitaline'll be dead if we let this thing hold us up for too long.

BEAR   I'm remembering....

CROW   Could you go a little faster?

BEAR   This one horned beast, she's a relative, part of us that was left behind long ago.

CROW   Well, it's great that Auntie Unicorn's come to pay a visit, but what about Jessica?

BEAR   [*to* UNICORN] I haven't seen you in such a long time....

CROW This is very touching, but....

BEAR I've wanted to see you and hear you.

WOLVERINE [*stalking the* UNICORN] And I've wanted to hear the sound of blood dripping on grass.... A spell made of unicorn spit. Taking us over, like they took us before ... piss on the white pockmarked ghosts in tall ships.

UNICORN [*holding her ground*] They took us all over. Remember that.

WOLVERINE They came in ships, so pretty and white, we were so generous, oh yes, no claws, no claws at all....
[WOLVERINE *swipes at* UNICORN, *who straddles him, holding the point of her horn against his throat*]

UNICORN I'm older than you. I can go all night. Suck you till you're mad.

VITALINE Grandmothers and Grandfathers!

BEAR The Crow is right, let Jessica speak.

VITALINE [*to* JESSICA] Open your heart to them, don't hold back. We're lucky they're listening at all, my old teacher would be having a fit by now....

JESSICA Grandmothers and Grandfathers, I see your colours, black, yellow, red, white.... I see the four directions, and I remember a long time ago when you asked me to sing, no, you told me I would be given a song, that I would find one.... But my throat closes off and chokes me, it's as if there is a stone in there and unless I let it loose, I'm going to die.... I'm not standing in a fertile place, I'm standing in a place that's dry and empty, like a desert. There are no leaves, the sun is covered in dust, everything is in a haze ... and when I throw my head back to ... to make the leaves come on the trees, there's nothing but a rasping sound, like death. I feel like an old withered pile of bones, I feel sucked dry. I've used and misused the gifts you've given me, and I've just come to an end. I can't go back and I can't go forward. Hear me, I'm asking you to help me.
[*The* SPIRITS *murmur in acknowledgement*]

CROW I've changed my mind. We accept the ceremony, and if 'Horny' here has any light to shed, we let her do her stuff. Jesse's stuck. She can't go forwards, and she can't go back. I say we take her back.

WOLVERINE She's failed, she should die by the roadside.

BEAR Jessica's never been able to balance us so far, and now there's one more. How do we know taking her back will make a difference?

UNICORN I'm what's been missing. Part of her power. Part of her blood.

CROW Jesse does have a foot in both camps ... so to speak.

VITALINE There's too many lying by the roadside! You have given her power. Just this once, if we could go farther, as far as she can go, as far as we can go....

CROW Just this once.

BEAR Wolverine?

WOLVERINE Hauggggghaughhh Aughhugghhhh zssssstttt!

BEAR [*acknowledges the vote*] Vitaline, this medicine lodge is as crazy as they come ... but we'll do as you ask, we'll take her back. Each one of us will come to her in our own time. She has to find a way to swallow what we have to teach. But you know the risk, power doesn't lie with us alone. As she goes backwards, you have to be the one to catch her, you have to keep her mind clear. It will be a shadow dream of what has happened.

VITALINE Jessica? The spirits are giving you a great gift. They're going to take you back. It will be very fast. Are you ready?
[JESSICA *nods*]

Peal of thunder.
Lights strobe,
revealing
Jessica curled on the floor,
six years old.

JESSICA [*as if asleep*] Mother? Ma? Where are you? I can't see you. I don't know where I am. It's cold and dark here. [*sings to comfort herself*] Tour a lour a laura, tour a lour a lie, tour a lour....
[VITALINE *pounds her cane on the ground.* JESSICA *jumps.* VITALINE *becomes* JESSICA's *grandmother,* KOOKOOM]
Kookoom? Grandma, where is she?

KOOKOOM / VITALINE Your mother has become one of the
    grandmothers and grandfathers.

JESSICA She's dead.

KOOKOOM / VITALINE You can still speak to her, she'll come to
    you in dreams.

JESSICA Dad's gonna get caught poaching, and they'll give us
    to the welfare people.

KOOKOOM / VITALINE I have something to show you. Look, it's a
    beautiful night.

    [*As she walks with* JESSICA, *powerful lights dance around
    them. The* SPIRITS *move with the light. The stars come
    down from the sky*]

KOOKOOM / VITALINE Like stars they come....
    their wings silver,
    their bodies shine.
    Listen, you can hear them....
    gossiping like women,
    sharing power,
    sisters and brothers of the earth.
    Pat the earth, stroke her,
    this woman is our Mother,
    we are her daughters and sons....
    There is an old man coming, old man
    to be your helper and show you the way....
    My grandmother passed him on to me,
    I pass him on to you....

    [*She waves a crow's wing, and* CROW *saunters on the
    scene*]

KOOKOOM / VITALINE He's not afraid of you. Talk to him, he's
    your guardian now.

JESSICA [*staring at* CROW] Will you be around all the time?

CROW Sort of.

JESSICA If the kids pick on me, will you get after them?

CROW Not exactly.

JESSICA Aren't you supposed to help me?

CROW I'm supposed to look out for you and teach you....

JESSICA How?

CROW Good question.

JESSICA Can you do magic? There's this girl at school, she's got
    blonde curly hair and white skin.

[UNICORN *reacts*] If I had a wish, I'd like to look like her.

CROW No direct interference. But you'll be out sometime, maybe in trouble, and you'll hear me whispering things, maybe things you don't want to hear. Spirits love giving hard advice. But I'm strong, handsome, I like horse races, gambling, I like to play pool, you want to learn to play pool? [*starts to show* JESSICA *some moves*]

KOOKOOM / VITALINE Hey, old Crow, she's too young for this gambling stuff.

CROW I'll be around. Sort of.

JESSICA Just don't leave me alone in the dark, okay?

CROW I don't make deals ... but it's a deal.

[CROW *struts away, returning to the watching* SPIRITS]

KOOKOOM / VITALINE Your spirits love you, always remember that.

Dark, twisted chords.
Jessica is suspended,
twelve years old.

[WOLVERINE *crawls toward* JESSICA]

CROW [*defensively*] You see? It wasn't such a bad childhood.

VITALINE You know what happened after....

CROW It was one of those things ... things like that happen, I mean, she didn't die, she was just....

[*As* JESSICA *speaks,* WOLVERINE *reaches out as if to unzip her pants*]

JESSICA [*seeing a stranger*] No, my dad's not here, nobody's home. You shouldn't just walk in like that.... I'm twelve, not sixteen.... Don't lie, I'm not all that pretty.... What are you doing?

[WOLVERINE *attacks*] Let go of me.... don't do that ... let go ... don't ... please....

[WOLVERINE *re-enacts the rape, grinding himself into the screaming girl*] ... don't do that ... ahh uhhh uhhhh nooooooo!

CROW [*shouts helplessly, as if he had the power to change the past*] Jesse! Run, get out of there ... just take off!

[JESSICA *lies sobbing.* WOLVERINE *crawls under*
VITALINE's *kitchen table.* UNICORN *is beside herself.*
BEAR *watches with understanding and grief.* CROW *tries*
to comfort JESSICA. *She shoves him away*]

VITALINE You were too late, Crow.

JESSICA [*in a broken voice, gaining strength*] Tour a lour a laura,
tour a lour a lye, tour a lour a laura, hush now don't
you cry.... [*she challenges her spirits*] Why couldn't you
help me? My spirits love me and not one of them
could help me. Why? Because you have no power. I
don't hear you, I don't see you, I'm blind. These aren't
green witch eyes, they're brown, do you hear me?
They're brown. I can make you die if I just close my
eyes.

Jimi Hendrix guitar sting.
Jessica is nineteen.
Vitaline transforms to Coyote,
as The Hotel Room appears.

[JESSICA *runs to The Hotel Room, ripping off her jeans and*
shirt as if they were burning her. Standing in her slip, she
stares at herself in a mirror]

CROW [*defensively*] It was a little hard to tell her Tinkerbell
was arriving soon to make it all better.

BEAR You want to make it too simple Crow. We have to
catch time now ... it's going to be hard for you,
Unicorn, are you ready?
[UNICORN *moves slowly, sensually toward The Hotel*
Room]

UNICORN I'll remind her of something, but she won't know
what. Something soft and strong and wild. A bit of the
goddess left over. I'll give her a feeling, just a feeling.
No matter what kind of hole she ends up in.

Unicorn lifts her mask,
raising it high into the air.
Coyote takes it, cradling it like a child.
Unicorn becomes Liz,
a high-class call girl.

[*A blast of music.* LIZ *enters The Hotel Room.* JESSICA
tries to deal with her hair. CROW *becomes the mirror*]

CROW I don't know what I'm going to do about my hair....

JESSICA [*to* LIZ, *ignoring* CROW] It was way up north, they
were going to put in electricity but they didn't get
around to it....

LIZ Use these. [*holds out ivory combs*] Pull your hair back to
make a chignon....

JESSICA A what?

CROW A chignon, you ignorant girl. It's French for, 'You're
getting into big trouble....'

JESSICA I can't hear you, remember?

LIZ Go for an oriental look, that's what Ellen wants.

JESSICA She said Chinese and Spanish, something exotic ...
that's what she said.

CROW Anything but Indian, no money in being an.... [*phony
war-woop*]

LIZ We're all a little exotic here, we like exotic names.
Flowers were big for a while, then one called Jasmine
lost her looks and ended up on the street.

JESSICA I couldn't see getting called Petunia Blossom or
anything like that....

LIZ Where did Ellen find you?

JESSICA My husband took me to this party just before he ran
off. I talked to Ellen and she had this look on her face,
then she gave me her number....

LIZ I've seen that look.... Put on some makeup.
[JESSICA *takes the makeup*]

CROW [*putting on his makeup*] Let's go home.

JESSICA I can't go home. Are you going to come up with the
rent money?

CROW That's not my department.

JESSICA You don't have a department....

LIZ Not like that, you look like a clown. Haven't you ever
worn blush before?

JESSICA Sure, just not this kind ... I was sort of a tomboy.
[LIZ *helps her*]
This is going to work out fine, I can tell, and if it
doesn't, that's okay too.

CROW It's the logic, the logic that gets to you.

JESSICA Gotta go fast, Crow, gobble it up. I'm not going to work like a dog and die young, like my mother. I'm going to get to Paris ... and ... Egypt. I'm going to have fifty pairs of shoes and eat in restaurants all the time. I'm going to know people with awards and degrees and mountains of books. I'm going to know things.

CROW Ask me, I know things.

JESSICA Not the things I want to know. Besides, I killed you ... remember?

[LIZ *brings out an expensive red dress and high heels. She helps* JESSICA *to dress*]

LIZ Ellen wants us to do doubles till you learn the ropes.

JESSICA What do we do?

LIZ Do?

JESSICA Like what?

LIZ You're not a virgin are you?

JESSICA Hell no, I have a kid and an ex-husband, I just married him to keep my brothers and sisters from getting thrown in foster homes but it didn't work. I don't even know where they are....

LIZ Look, I left the violin at home. You getting cold feet?

JESSICA After my husband, it's not my feet that are cold.

LIZ [*warming up a bit*] Close your eyes and think of Victorian porn, or the money. Two hundred dollars a man ain't bad....

CROW Two hundred bucks! No, that's good, that's really pretty good.

LIZ But you have to be careful, a lot of them are politicians, business men, men with power.

CROW A certain kind of power.

JESSICA High class....

LIZ To men, high class is quiet, so look great and only talk about them. These guys are under a lot of pressure, and all of a sudden they can't get off the way they used to. But the wife only knows one position, so they come to us. We're not afraid of a few kinks to help them out. They want beauty when they come to you. Beauty with clear eyes and no problems.

JESSICA As long as they take their boots off and they don't wear red.

LIZ You never know....

JESSICA And they're not too tall....

LIZ Why?

JESSICA I got raped by a mountie when I was twelve....
[*The* SPIRITS *move in, beginning to take focus*]

CROW Every time she mentions it I feel sick.... What could I do? It wasn't my fault, I was at the race track, but....

LIZ My stepfather did it to me when I was ten, but he took his shoes off....

CROW Now I'm really going to be sick....

JESSICA Liz?

LIZ Don't talk.

Liz transforms to Unicorn.
She must convince the Native Spirits
to draw power
from another time,
another kind of source.

UNICORN Just give in a little, give her a chance. You have to feel the Lady. Like silk between your thighs.

CROW What's so holy about being a hooker?

UNICORN They could heal with their mouths, hands, tongues....

COYOTE I'm starting to remember....

CROW There's too much remembering going on.

BEAR The idea is to take away shame.

CROW Who's ashamed?

COYOTE Jessica's ashamed.

CROW She didn't get that from me.

WOLVERINE She chose to be a whore. Let her pray to Ishtar and have done with it.

UNICORN [*surprised, turning to* WOLVERINE] You do remember.

BEAR Jessica's learning according to some pretty crazy traditions, but at least it's tradition.

CROW All right, maybe I'm remembering and maybe I'm not, let's just do it.

Raunchy music.
Unicorn transforms to Liz.
Bear transforms into a naive gorfy client.
Crow transforms into a gorfy elegant client.

[*Lights up on The Hotel Room.* LIZ, JESSICA, *and the two* CLIENTS *find themselves in the middle of an awkward party*]

JESSICA I'm still hungry, I want more avacado and shrimp.

LIZ [*aside to* JESSICA] Watch the drinking, we haven't started work yet and I don't know what these guys are into....

CLIENT / CROW [*trying on a slight British accent*] More champagne?

LIZ Hey, why aren't you drinking?

CLIENT / CROW We don't drink, but don't hold it against us....

LIZ I'm ready to hold something against you....

CLIENT / BEAR What's your name again?

LIZ Camillia, do you like it?

CLIENT / CROW No no, your name should be from the ancients, Ishtar, or Gaia or Tana....

LIZ I'll take Tana, that sounds Irish....

JESSICA I'm Irish ... Irish, Scots and French and....

CLIENT / CROW And what?

JESSICA Spanish.

LIZ This kind of talk gets her all hot and bothered, right Jasmine?

JESSICA What? Yeah, hot and bothered....

CLIENT / BEAR [*as if he's just learned his lines*] Ishtar, the uh, round-bellied ... goddess, who is the Mother, who is the beginning....

LIZ Watch it, I've been doing my sit-ups....

CLIENT / BEAR You're a healer and you don't know it....

CLIENT / CROW A priestess ... a priestess and a healer....

CLIENT / BEAR A healer and a priestess....

CLIENT / CROW So true ... so true.... They don't know, do they?

CLIENT / BEAR No, they don't.

LIZ Know what?

CLIENT / CROW Why is it the oldest profession?

LIZ Why?

CLIENT / CROW You'll see. You think you're doing something bad. But in ancient times, when the round-bellied goddess ruled....

LIZ I know, why don't we all take a bath together? This room has one of those great big tubs....

JESSICA Good idea, I'm just dying to take my clothes off and have some fun with you guys.... [*to* LIZ] They're weirdos....

LIZ This is nothing.

CLIENT / CROW Ahh yes, the ritual cleansing.

CLIENT / BEAR A lost tradition ... a path of giving....

JESSICA Let's keep tradition out of this, okay?

LIZ She just means, that kind of talk turns her off a bit....

CLIENT / BEAR There was wildness and lunacy and ecstacy.... What's wild deserves to live, otherwise we're all....

CLIENT / CROW Imagine no hiding, no shame, the cycles in their place. The goddess smiles, as men, soiled by war, come to the temple to be purged and healed, their sacred juices mingling ... cleansed, not dirtied, by their special arts....

CLIENT / BEAR Mingling the juices with the juices....

LIZ Why don't we do that right now ... you're so juicy you're driving me wild....

JESSICA Let's not talk so much.

BEAR / CLIENT First, the prayers.

JESSICA What prayers?

CLIENT / CROW The ritual prayers before the act....

LIZ All you're getting is the act....

CLIENT / BEAR The prayers make the act more beautiful....

LIZ Who says it's beautiful?

JESSICA No praying, that's final.

LIZ If you don't believe in anything, you can't pray....

CLIENT / BEAR We're born knowing how to pray.

JESSICA No.

CLIENT / CROW [*counting out a large roll of bills*] It's a loose sort of thing, best done outside or in a dark room. Just tune in to that great big 'she' out there. No big deal. Now where was I? Oh yes, two hundred, that's above what we already paid you, three hundred, four hundred, five hundred....

CLIENT / BEAR Five hundred.

JESSICA No.

CLIENT / CROW Eight hundred, nine hundred, one thousand.

LIZ Each?

CLIENT / BEAR Each.

LIZ You're on.

JESSICA No.

CLIENT / CROW Then I'll double it, that's a final offer....

LIZ [*capitulating*] I was brought up by priests, there was this one old guy who used to burn himself with a candle to show us the pain of hell. I could do him....

CROW No pain, only pleasure.

CLIENT / BEAR Here are the blindfolds....

LIZ No you don't.

CLIENT / CROW [*to* JESSICA] Praying is listening, and at these prices....

[JESSICA *almost recognizes* CROW]

LIZ They'll take the money and beat us to a pulp....

JESSICA [*staring at* CROW] No they won't.

[CROW *and* BEAR *blindfold the girls*]

LIZ [*to* JESSICA] If we get out of this alive, this round-bellied goddess is going to be after your ass.

[JESSICA *and* LIZ *start to giggle nervously*]

CLIENT / CROW Let's go girls, think deep down, right from that female plumbing. It's like a sing-a-long, just repeat after me. [*chants*] Ishtar....

JESSICA Never heard of her.

LIZ I have a feeling you will.... [*more giggles*]

CLIENT / CROW Come on girls.... Iiiiishtar....

JESSICA / LIZ Eeeeeshshshtar....

BEAR / CROW Aaaaastaaarte.... Aaaaaltaaaar....

JESSICA / LIZ Ishtar.... Astarte.... Altar....

BEAR / CROW Innanna.... Morrigana.... Mari....

Soft drumming,
a memory of
the Goddess chant
takes over them all.

[COYOTE *and* WOLVERINE *join in a weave of elongated sounds*]

JESSICA / LIZ / SPIRITS Innanna, Morrigana ... Mari ... Ishtar ... Astarte ... Altar ... Innanna ... Morrigana ... Mari....

[CROW *and* BEAR *draw away. Throughout the 'whore's*

prayer', the SPIRITS *chant softly.* LIZ *and* JESSICA, *caught in the spell, try to break it]*

LIZ This goddess has too many names for her own good.

JESSICA A great big 'she' out there. Like hell. What's she think she's been doing all this time?

LIZ She expects to be talked to like she stayed around to watch.

JESSICA She says,'Sorry girls, times were hard and I had to cut out.'

[*In the back of her mind* LIZ *remembers the* UNICORN]

LIZ She says she's been around ... kind of sleeping ... whispering and ... spinning threads....

JESSICA I don't feel any threads.

LIZ I do.

JESSICA Then what's she look like?

[*They are beginning to touch each other's hair, joking still, but the tenor has changed]*

LIZ Humungous thighs, hips like the side of a truck, big floppy stomach, breasts like torpedoes....

JESSICA Long long hair....

LIZ And big weird eyes, lots of liner, green shadow....

JESSICA But like a cat, not afraid of the dark....

LIZ Not afraid of anything ... she's easy....

[*They are lightly sexual]*

JESSICA So easy she kind of slides. Then she laughs....

LIZ Then she cries....

JESSICA Then she dances like a crazy thing....

LIZ What about him?

JESSICA He's a hunter, wild like her ... he picks her up in his arms....

LIZ He's always dying and getting born again....

JESSICA He's the biggest greatest man....

LIZ And she's the biggest greatest woman, and they have fantastic sex all the time....

JESSICA And she always comes....

LIZ And he always knows when....

[*They are laughing and rocking in each other's arms]*

JESSICA He's her son, and her lover, and her king....

[*The* SPIRITS' *chant builds]*

LIZ She's the earth and the moon and the grandmother.
She's the goddess that farts and eats, who gets mad,
then loves, who knows all the rhythms and all the
changes, who changes and changes....

JESSICA Who is freeee....

LIZ Who is freeeeee....

JESSICA Who is freeyyyyyyyyayyyyyyyahhhhhh heyyyahhh ...

LIZ ... hhhhhhaheyyyyahhhhhhhh....

[JESSICA *and* LIZ *are in a kind of ecstacy.* LIZ *drops back,
letting* JESSICA's *voice rise. Suddenly* JESSICA *cuts out,
yanking off her blindfold*]

LIZ [*betrayed*] Why'd you stop?

JESSICA Why'd you stop?

LIZ I stopped because you stopped....

JESSICA You didn't have to stop because I did....

LIZ It's your fucking song....

JESSICA You didn't grow up with it like I did.

LIZ They pay extra for innocence, but it only lasts so long,
remember that.

*Liz transforms to Unicorn.
Jessica paces The Hotel Room.
Unicorn paces,
confused, defeated.*

COYOTE [*helpfully*] That was pretty good, almost worked.

BEAR It was too soon.

CROW It was too weird.

COYOTE It was too much fun, Jesse doesn't like fun.

CROW Of course she likes fun. I'm fun, and if I like fun, she
likes fun. I'm having fun right now.

WOLVERINE She couldn't stand her tests. I've seen them shredded
to bits and still smiling.

UNICORN [*realizing, almost to herself*] All of a sudden there was
good and evil and they were in different places ...
that's why she couldn't....

WOLVERINE [*explodes*] She needs to see the other side. I'll show her.
I'll teach her about Ishtar.

[WOLVERINE *darts to The Hotel Room, slavering.* CROW
stops him just in time]

CROW Oh no you don't.

WOLVERINE Then who will?

CROW I will.

> *Crow rips off his feathers,*
> *Transforming to the Weird Client.*
> *He offers his mask to Wolverine.*
> *Wolverine accepts it.*

WOLVERINE Hauhhahhhhhggg.

> *Unicorn transforms to Liz.*
> *Coyote starts to cry.*

> [*Focus shifts to The Hotel Room*]

BEAR Too much has been taken from Jessica. She needs some loving that isn't part of the bargain.

WOLVERINE There's no such thing.
[LIZ *throws herself on the hotel room floor, writhing and moaning dramatically.* JESSICA *ties the* WEIRD CLIENT *to a chair*]

WEIRD CLIENT [*mean*] Tie me tighter, you bitch. Say it again.

LIZ I'm a piece of shit....

WEIRD CLIENT Know nothing, are nothing, dirty, filthy full of bugs....

LIZ Know nothing....

WEIRD CLIENT Not you, her.... [*meaning* JESSICA]
[COYOTE *watches, her crying intensifies*]

JESSICA Why won't she stop crying?

LIZ She's always liked the sound of her own crying ... it's your turn....

JESSICA [*lies down at* CROW'*s feet*] This is different.

WEIRD CLIENT Say it.

JESSICA [*begins writhing like* LIZ] Know nothing, am nothing, dirty filthy....

WEIRD CLIENT Dirty, filthy, redskin squaw. Ha! Didn't think I knew?

LIZ [*to* JESSICA] Just put the toothpaste in your mouth and get on with it....

JESSICA I'll say it. Dirty, filthy, redskin squaw....

WEIRD CLIENT My wife doesn't live with me anymore ... tie me
tighter....
[LIZ *is about to climb on* CROW's *face*]
LIZ [*to* JESSICA] You do the bottom, I'll do the top.
[COYOTE's *crying gets louder, more desperate. The music
twists and whines*]
JESSICA [*doesn't know this routine*] You mean ...?
WEIRD CLIENT [*hoarsely*] Whores of Babylon, soiled with filth.
JESSICA [*coming apart*] I can't do it....
LIZ [*tough*] Hold the toothpaste in your mouth, kneel
down....
JESSICA Why is she still crying?

Coyote is sobbing,
Bear prowls back and forth,
Crow is panting, desperate,
Wolverine hisses.
They drive the pressure.

WEIRD CLIENT Hurry, hurry, don't let me down.
LIZ [*urgently to* JESSICA] Just do it....
[JESSICA *puts the toothpaste in her mouth and kneels
down. She gags and throws up all over* CROW's *crotch. The
crying stops dead*]
JESSICA I'm sorry ... I....
WEIRD CLIENT Don't talk. That was ... the most incredible
experience of my life.
LIZ Do you want us to clean you up?
WEIRD CLIENT No need, just cut me loose and I'll be on my
way....
JESSICA I've got to see why she stopped crying. [*runs off*]
WEIRD CLIENT [*to* LIZ] I'm in love. She's so spontaneous.
[LIZ *unties his bonds*]
Do I have to pay extra for that?
LIZ Consider it a gift.
WEIRD CLIENT Same time next week?
LIZ You bet.
WEIRD CLIENT Salut.
[CROW *rejoins the* SPIRITS. LIZ *takes out needles and
heroin.* JESSICA *walks slowly into The Hotel Room*]

JESSICA She's dead.

LIZ You're lucky, he could've killed us....

JESSICA The girl in the room next door.

LIZ I heard you. [*she shoots up*] You knew something was up, didn't you? You should tell fortunes....

JESSICA I've been hearing her for weeks, I could've gone over with a bottle of scotch one night....

LIZ No you couldn't.... [*suddenly to* JESSICA] We're not friends.

JESSICA What do you mean?

LIZ We're just not friends.
[WOLVERINE *crawls behind the mirror, playing* JESSICA's *reflection*]

JESSICA I'm starting to get ugly, aren't I? I'm doing too much. I'm losing my looks.

LIZ Relax. [*hands* JESSICA *the stuff*]

JESSICA I'd kill myself if I didn't have a kid.

LIZ No you wouldn't.

JESSICA [*shooting up*] She's in a convent. The nuns are looking after her, can you believe it?

LIZ Priestesses....

JESSICA Don't start that again.

LIZ Okay.

JESSICA You got any kids?

LIZ I don't remember.

JESSICA You suck me in and then you cut me off.

LIZ There's one thing we're not going to do. We're not going to get a box of man-sized kleenex and tell each other the truth.

JESSICA [*feeling the heroin*] Here she comes ...

LIZ ... in rainbow colours....

JESSICA Lady H, she is so beautiful....

LIZ She is, but there's nothing like the first time.

JESSICA After that, you've always got your hand out....

LIZ But she dances away with that tinkling laugh....

JESSICA Did that goddess stuff make any sense to you?
[LIZ *turns on* JESSICA]

LIZ People like you only go so far down, then you use something in your back pocket....

JESSICA People like me?

LIZ You're going to get out of here.

JESSICA You're the one who's white, you could get out anytime.

LIZ [*cruel*] I'm a squaw, I don't know anything. Oooooh, look at that electricity....

JESSICA You could do anything you wanted, and you blew it.

LIZ You know what you're scared of? Magic. [*pushes her*]

JESSICA [*pushing her back*] You don't know what you're talking about.

LIZ [*wrangling*] No real guts, you've got no real guts.

JESSICA You like to set yourself up, all high and mighty, the know-all whore....

LIZ What about Ishtar, Jesse?

JESSICA I think she needs a new name.

LIZ Like what?

JESSICA I don't know, Petunia Blossom or something like that....
[*They are suddenly still and distant*] I don't think I can keep it up any longer....

LIZ So stop.

JESSICA Where are you going?

LIZ If I had the kind of electricity around me that you have, I wouldn't be shooting the Lady. I'd be talking to her.

Liz transforms to Unicorn.
Raw discordant strings.
The Spirits zero in.
Jessica is again drawn to the mirror.
Wolverine is behind it.

JESSICA You should be able to see it, that's the trouble, it should show. A big bloody hole with guts coming out. It used to feel like I got shot, now it feels more like a horse kicked me. I'm doubled up and I'm never going to get undoubled. It's got to show, got to make some blood at least....
[WOLVERINE *thrusts a knife towards her*]

WOLVERINE Yaughhhhghhhhhahhhhh....
[*Dreamlike,* JESSICA *takes the knife.* COYOTE *bangs the ground, looking frantically for* CROW. CROW *crawls into*

The Hotel Room seconds before JESSICA *cuts herself. He makes a death rattle sound*]

JESSICA What's that? My soul talking?

CROW You don't have a soul.

JESSICA Yes I do.

CROW You make me puke.

JESSICA You make me puke, you going to play tough?

CROW Let's play both ends of the stick, see how quick we can get to the middle, let's play tough bitch and stupid chick, let's play hooker and junkie and Halfbreed from the bush, see how quick you can kill us both. I can't even fly anymore, I had to crawl here all the way from the pool hall.

JESSICA Is it true I don't have a soul?

CROW A little one, about the size of a pimple, one good squeeze and it's gone.

JESSICA Then give me some advice.

CROW Drink light beer instead of whisky.

JESSICA I want to die....

CROW You think if you die, you stop dreaming?

JESSICA It has to show, I just have to cut myself ... see, I'll make a ritual out of it, I'll offer the blood to the grandmothers and grandfathers....
[*The* SPIRITS *zap* JESSICA *hard. She doubles over*]

CROW You deserved that.

JESSICA [*facing them down*] You want me to act like someone with power? Okay. If I say I'm going to cut myself for the grandmothers....
[*The* SPIRITS *gather closer*]

CROW What's your reason?

JESSICA I don't know ... my grandmother told me that in the Sun Dance the bones cut through you, you pulled against the ropes, danced through your pain ... your suffering was for something....

BEAR But Jessica, do you want to suffer?

JESSICA No, I just have to cut myself ... have to see something....

UNICORN You can see without taking a knife to yourself.

CROW I thought you were trying to kill yourself.

JESSICA Not really....

COYOTE You can't make a flesh offering to the spirits unless you know why, and it has to be done with joy....

WOLVERINE You have to have a reason, what's your reason, Jessica, what's your vow?

BEAR If you want to die, then die, but an offering has to do with life.

COYOTE What's your reason?

JESSICA I want to know what was supposed to happen, I want to know what I was supposed to be when I was first dreamed.... [*offers the knife to* CROW] Crow, you do it.
[CROW *takes the knife, holds it above* JESSICA'*s arm*]

CROW Deep or shallow?

JESSICA Do you think I love suffering too much?

CROW Yes. Deep or shallow?

JESSICA Deep.
[*Strobe blackout*]

Coyote transforms to Vitaline.
Jessica speaks as though
entranced,
while Crow leads her to The Looney Bin.

JESSICA All she knew is that she was walking. She was tired and she was walking across empty plains.
[*In The Looney Bin,* CROW *puts* JESSICA *in a straight jacket, then helps himself to a doctor's coat*]
She walked because she had to tell them something, she had to remind them. She didn't want to be the one that had to come, she had begged to stay, but now she was trapped in a human body....

Unicorn transforms to Liz.
Vitaline hands Liz a small bag.
Wolverine tries to enter The Looney Bin,
Bear stops him.

[JESSICA *sits motionless in a chair.* CROW *stands protectively behind her.* LIZ *enters, acting nonchalant*]

LIZ You're looking pretty good for somebody that went off the deep end.... Did you hear we got raided?
Ellen's in jail, I've had it, I'm quitting the business.

JESSICA   She was so tired, she could hardly remember where she had come from. Finally, when she could barely stand, she saw two hunters coming towards her....

LIZ   I went looking for your money and all I found was a hundred dollars, but don't worry, the kid's in a foster home, you just have to prove you're normal to get her back. Good luck.

[JESSICA *doesn't acknowledge* LIZ, *but continues the story of the White Buffalo Calf Woman*]

JESSICA   Then the hunters saw she was wearing the head of a white buffalo calf. As they came near, she knew one of them wanted to rape her, and the other recognized her. She let one come very close, willing him to stop. He reached out to grab her, she looked into eyes that had never been taught, then a cloud rose up, and he became dust.

LIZ   Are you on shock treatments or pills, or what? I wouldn't mind some of those pills. Knock-knock? I have to go, I'm seeing somebody who's going to help me kick....

JESSICA   [*connects with* LIZ] Cold turkey?

LIZ   Like the day after Thanksgiving. You're going to get out of here, you know that. Oh, I got you a little something. [LIZ *puts a stuffed unicorn in* JESSICA's *lap*] See you.

Liz becomes Unicorn.
The Spirits gather round Vitaline.

JESSICA   [*continues the story*] She told the other hunter to go ahead and prepare the camp. As she watched him go, she knew she was on the brink of what all the suffering had been for, and for the first time, she was afraid. She asked them why, when she was so close, should she shake with fear? Then she saw a starling fly across her path, guiding her to the camp.... They're not kind, but they know a lot.

[VITALINE *smashes her stick on the ground*]

VITALINE   She needs some loving that isn't part of the bargain....

CROW   It's time for the Bear.

The lazy whine
of a harmonica.
Bear is asleep in a corner.
Crow wakes him up.
Bear transforms to Sam.

CROW Sam?

SAM [*growling*] What?

CROW Sam, wake up, we're going to meet a lady.

SAM I don't like ladies ... and I've got a hell of a hangover....

CROW [*dragging* SAM *to The Looney Bin*] Now don't get put off by the atmosphere, she's a special girl, a bit off her food maybe, but give her an open stretch of track and you can bet on the nose.

SAM I don't like horse traders....

CROW Just a gambler....
[*They enter The Looney Bin,* JESSICA *sits staring into space*] Hey, Jesse, you've got to meet Sam, he goes to the same bars as....

SAM [*intrigued*] Hi, Jesse.
[JESSICA *is oblivious*]

CROW [*hustling*] He's an organizer, Red Power, the whole deal....

SAM I can bet I can tell why you're in here.

CROW Because she's crazy....

JESSICA Because I'm crazy....

SAM No, because you're oppressed.

CROW Best opening line I've heard in a year....

SAM It's true. The crazy houses and penetentiaries are full of our people.

JESSICA She was so tired....

SAM Look at it this way. We've been murdered, starved, raped and pillaged. When that didn't work they infected us with diseases, fed us booze and made us dependent on handouts. They stole our land, broke up our families, outlawed our language and religion, and worst of all, they spent a lot of money making terrible movies about us. We're outlaws, and if we can admit that, we can fight back.

JESSICA All you can do is try to survive....

SAM And be an Uncle Tomahawk?

CROW That's great, he's got a great sense of humour....

SAM You don't just have to survive, you can stand up.
Can't you feel the wind changing?

JESSICA What wind?

SAM Everybody has the right to food, shelter, clothing, and
when the work is done, to something beautiful. You
know you're beautiful don't you?

CROW Well, if I lost a few pounds, and got a good haircut....

SAM [*to* CROW] Don't you have to go somewhere?

CROW I don't think so.

SAM Think harder.
[CROW *and* BEAR *speak spirit to spirit*]

CROW You're taking her away from me.

BEAR Nobody can do that.

CROW As a matter of fact, I have to go see a man about a
bear.... See you, Jesse, I'll be around, sort of....
[CROW *struts away to join* UNICORN, WOLVERINE *and*
VITALINE]

As Crow gives way,
real time appears to take over
from memory.
The ceremony becomes more
seductive.
Bear begins to lose himself.
Jessica believes what she sees.

SAM Does all this sound like bullshit to you?

JESSICA I don't know.

SAM I was in the pen for quite a while, I know what it's like
to be locked up.... Ask me what I did.

JESSICA What did you do?

SAM I read books. I read about the Black Panthers, the
unions, I even read about the French Revolution. I got
blown away. I started asking myself why we couldn't
do something, instead of rotting on our knees....

JESSICA We don't know who 'we' is.

SAM 'We' is Native people. Or maybe not, maybe 'we' is
anybody with a pure heart.

JESSICA I'm a Halfbreed.

SAM Then you've got too much heart.... Join up with us, what've you got to lose? You have a place to go?

JESSICA No.

SAM Any money?

JESSICA No.

SAM Somebody to look after you?

JESSICA No.

SAM Son of a bitch, you must be oppressed.

JESSICA I have a kid in a foster home, I'm four months pregnant, and I don't like sex.

SAM I love women with problems. In case you didn't notice, I'm making an offer.

JESSICA I said I don't like it.

SAM Then you don't have to ... I won't touch you.

JESSICA [*with some humour*] I don't think that's possible....

SAM It's just like wrestling, you used to be a tomboy, didn't you?

JESSICA I puke if someone touches me now ... I puke and fight like a mad dog....

SAM Come here....

JESSICA Don't you want to know who the father is?

SAM Come here, baby, come here.

[*kisses her, she kisses back for a long time*]

Let's get out of here.

JESSICA What did you say your name was?

SAM Gabriel Dumont.

[SAM *and* JESSICA *exit. The* SPIRITS *watch closely*]

CROW She's out of our hands now.

COYOTE It's going to seem real for her now.

UNICORN Real and not real.

WOLVERINE Just keep her alive for me.

[*Blackout, end of Act One*]

Act Two

VITALINE *sits in her kitchen, smoking. In the apartment,*
JESSICA *types awkwardly at an old portable machine. A*
stuffed unicorn sits in a high chair, books and papers are
piled on the floor. SAM *is stretched out on the couch,*
fiddling with his guitar.

Wolverine, Unicorn and Crow
saunter into the apartment.
Casual now, a part of the furniture,
Wolverine coils around the phone.

[SAM *and* JESSICA *have been trying to fill out grant*
application forms. It isn't easy]

JESSICA [*reading*] 'Describe the function of your project and
how it relates to the previous criteria.'

SAM [*by heart*] 'If your project does not relate to the
previous criteria, explain why, using box number
three or four-B.' We've got too much damn criteria,
they only give you two lines.

JESSICA [*slinking over to* SAM] If box number three or four-B is
unable to contain your expectations, remove clothes
slowly and gobble up the man on your right.

SAM Who's the guy on your right? I'm the guy on your left.

JESSICA Too far left, that's your problem.

SAM I don't have any problems.

JESSICA If you hadn't formed the Association we wouldn't
have to do this.

SAM You're the only woman I could ever stand nagging
me.

Wolverine stirs,
Vitaline leans forward,
Crow and Unicorn leap up.

[*The phone rings.* SAM *and* JESSICA *go cold*]

SAM [*tense*] I'll get it.

JESSICA No, I'll get it.
[WOLVERINE *hands her the phone*]

Hello? Who is this? You're going to have to talk
louder ... yes, I do. [*she hangs up, shaken*]

SAM [*angry*] Who was it?

JESSICA It doesn't matter. You hungry?

SAM Don't give me that, who was it?

JESSICA I can heat up those fish sticks in the freezer, and
there's leftover salad....

SAM Who was it?

JESSICA It was just one of those calls.

SAM Same guy?

JESSICA Sounded like a different voice. 'Do you know where
your children are?' Like out of the spy movies. Then
he said, 'You better quit making trouble or start
worrying every time they leave the house.'

SAM Kids in bed?

JESSICA Maybe I should check on them, just to be....

SAM [*quietly*] Do you want to quit?
[SAM *and* JESSICA *face each other*]

JESSICA No.

SAM It's going to get heavier.

JESSICA I'll bet it gets easier.

SAM Maybe you're right. If we can figure out how to play
the right hand of the political wing, we can get fifty,
maybe a hundred thousand dollars of government
money.

JESSICA Half for the halfway house?

SAM We have to work it out. After that, you're home free.
You get your first bunch of money from Ottawa, and it
keeps coming, because you're on their books.

JESSICA That's not what you wanted.

SAM Of course not. I wanted us to ride to Ottawa, in full
battle gear, make a ring around the peace tower, shoot
the fuckers down, and tell them where to dump their
uranium. But it didn't work out like that.

JESSICA Maybe there's other ways of doing it.

SAM Sure, one of these days we'll sit down with the Big
Blue Machine, and the Big Red Machine, and maybe
even the N.D.P., and we'll order a big fancy dinner
and tell 'em what we want. And we'll have money
and paper behind us. They like lots of paper.

JESSICA I mean like Big Bear used to do it. He could waste his enemies at a hundred yards. Put up walls of smoke, give 'em bad dreams.

SAM Those government guys don't dream, they just lie down and balance the budget.

The sound of pipes.
Vitaline walks slowly
to the ceremony circle.
Jessica stares into space,
drifting toward the Spirits.

SAM Hey, earth to Jesse, come in please.

JESSICA Sorry....

SAM Where were you?

JESSICA You know....

SAM I keep forgetting, you're as crazy as a hoot owl....
[JESSICA *spaces out again*]
Jesse?

JESSICA There's a room, it's the room I can't get out of my head.... I remember an old woman and a room, then it's black and I see a green flash of light.... It gets louder, everything pounding at once.... I feel so light ... there's wind ... and the flash of light ... they're telling me to ... go....

The Spirits focus on Vitaline.
The ceremony is exhausting her.
She reaches out in a moment
of despair.

VITALINE Grandmothers and Grandfathers, hear this Coyote woman. Thunder beings, spirits of fire, earth, air and sea. Where are our prayers when the earth is covered and hidden? When we no longer see you, when you are pushed farther and farther away? They tell me the earth our mother is a bomb that will burn my lungs and flesh. They tell me that she is not our mother. That she has no more children to bear. Give me the strength to dig deep, to say, 'No! There is power that will save us.' Let me teach her well, let me teach her well.

Vitaline releases the Spirits.
The Spirits release Jessica.
Dazed, she returns to the
reality
of the apartment.

SAM [*to* JESSICA] Come here. [*He holds her*] You've done enough drugs in your time to give you flashbacks till you're ninety ... just come back....

JESSICA I'm sorry....

SAM Don't be sorry....

JESSICA I wish I was normal....

SAM I'd trade you in if you were.

JESSICA Do you want something to eat?

SAM I can't keep up.... Green Eyes. First time I saw those eyes I couldn't believe it.

JESSICA Irish.

SAM Full of the Blarney Stone. You're getting pretty mouthy at the meetings.

JESSICA I can't help it. It took me all this time to realize those guys aren't smarter than me.

SAM You're smarter than the lot of them.
[JESSICA *turns away*]
Here we go, you've got that look on your face, like nothing's pure enough for you.

JESSICA [*hot*] What about this look?

SAM That's different.

JESSICA What does it say?

SAM It says, I'm your Iroquois brave and you're my vermin-infested Halfbreed, gambling away the profits and fiddling at the moon.

JESSICA What else?

SAM It says, 'Time for the Bear.'
[VITALINE *pounds her cane on floor*]

VITALINE I don't think so, I think it's time for the Coyote.

Vitaline becomes Coyote.
Jessica is suspended.
Sam transforms to Bear.
The Spirits take over.

CROW [*announcer voice*] She's prime, she's chafing at the bit, I've got money on this one and she's coming into the home stretch, the crowd's cheering, they can't believe it, she's flying across the finish line.

COYOTE The Coyote woman is ready, we all know that.

CROW If we're taking her back, we can change a few things, Vitaline's too set in the old ways, we need someone who understands the new modern woman.

UNICORN We need someone who can turn flame into a torch.

COYOTE Vitaline's crawled under fences, stolen chickens, even dressed up at the Calgary Stampede, she'll do anything to survive. She'll know what to do with Jesse.

WOLVERINE I know what to do with Jesse. Give her to me. She's losing her scent, she's got no anger left, give her to me.

CROW She's not ready for you yet.
[BEAR *blocks* WOLVERINE *with difficulty*]

BEAR Wait, Wolverine, your time is coming.
[WOLVERINE *stalks, jaws open*]

WOLVERINE Just keep her alive for me.

BEAR Is the Coyote woman ready?

COYOTE The Coyote woman is ready.

Whirring sounds.
Coyote transforms to Vitaline.
Jessica is drawn
to Vitaline's cabin.

VITALINE [*puttering in her kitchen*] Let me teach her well.

JESSICA [*climbing to the cabin*] Hello? Anybody home? [*She enters the kitchen.* VITALINE *seems to appear out of thin air*] Oh, sorry to barge in. When I asked in town, they told me to come here. Are you Vitaline?

VITALINE Sometimes they call me that, sometimes they don't. [*hands* JESSICA *a cup of her terrible coffee*] Jessica.

JESSICA That's right. How did you....

VITALINE Us old women, we don't know too much, but every once in a while, something clicks.

JESSICA My family used to live around here, but I'm not sure where ... my grandmother married a Thompson and my father was a.... [*she stops suddenly*] This is the house isn't it? The first one, when my mother was alive. I remember it now.

VITALINE Don't get too dramatic.

JESSICA My grandmother used to sit over there.

VITALINE I knew her.

JESSICA I don't remem....

VITALINE Your memory's not so good, but we'll fix that. Next time you come you'll wear a skirt and we'll start. I don't know what's going on these days, all the women running around like they got something long between their legs. You've got something ... but it's not that long.

JESSICA It'll probably be a while before I come up again. It's a long drive and....

VITALINE You'll wear a skirt, and we'll start. You going to tell me you don't know what I'm talking about?

JESSICA I'd love to tell you I don't know what you're talking about.

[CROW *sneaks in closer*]

VITALINE I saw that Crow of yours today, he's flapping around acting like he's a big shot but he isn't. He's gonna lose his beak soon, and so are you, if you don't start learning.

JESSICA I'm not ready yet.

VITALINE You're never ready. You think I was ready? The first time I called the spirits, I peed my pants.

JESSICA The first time I called them I was at the race track.

VITALINE Okay, I'm going to teach you about a certain kind of power. [*as if by rote*] 'Before the French and the English, even before the Irish, even before the Cree and the Blackfoot, there was the Mother, the Old Woman....'

JESSICA [*interrupting*] Does this have something to do with a round-bellied goddess?

VITALINE You're going to end up with a round-bellied kick in the pants if you don't watch it.... [*motions for* JESSICA *to follow her outside*] When I was young, people were still visiting each other without their bodies. That's 'astral projection', a university guy taught me that,

but he wasn't so smart. I told him it was a practical
thing, if you were out hunting, and you got in trouble,
you'd send out your thoughts. If nobody was
listening, then you started praying.

JESSICA   I've been scared to come here all this time, and now it
doesn't seem so bad.

VITALINE   You waited a long time to come, too much longer and
you wouldn't be able to see them anymore.

JESSICA   I can still see them.

VITALINE   That's what I said, you can still see them. I can make
the Northern Lights come down.

JESSICA   Anybody can do that just by whistling.

VITALINE   You're going to be dangerous when you learn.

JESSICA   My grandmother used to make the stars come down.

VITALINE   Just like the Christians, always wanting proof, a little
miracle or something.... Let's see what I can do. Look
up.

Waves of chanting, flutes.
Vitaline transforms to Coyote.
The stars come down from the sky.
The Spirits gather close.
Jessica remembers.

VITALINE   That's pretty good, eh?

JESSICA   No more trying to be normal, no more pushing them
away. I'll walk into Safeway, feeling them at the
checkout counter: '*TV Guide*, six chocolate bars, four
packages of gum, and some tobacco for that Bear
behind your head.'

Hard metallic whines.
The apartment world cuts through.
Coyote transforms to Vitaline.

[CROW *staggers into the apartment half carrying* SAM,
who's drunk]

SAM   We're drinking tonight,
for a change, for a change,
we're drinking tonight for a change.
We're drinking the tears
of a thousand years,

we're drinking tonight for a change.
We watch them pass down like a waterfall,
From generation, drop.
Generation, drop,
generation, drop.
Catch.
We're drinking tonight for a change.
Remembering. Remembering. Remembering.
Remembering the taste and the sound and the smell,
drinking tonight to remember
and feel and dwell and wallow....
think of all the times,
all the runs all the chases
as we crawl through the bushes and watch and cry,
as we crawl, as we fight, as we crawl
on our bellies and watch and see....
we're remembering things tonight.
[CROW *begins to dance to* SAM's *rhythm*]
We're remembering battles when we lost
and we lost and we lost and we lost.
We're remembering battles
where we had a good time,
and we lost and we lost and we lost....
We're remembering the day when he said,
'No, let us pray.'
And we said,
'No, let us fight.'
[SAM *passes out and* CROW *covers him tenderly with a blanket*]

Lightning quick,
Wolverine moves toward Jessica,
The other Spirits back away.

WOLVERINE Let her see what she hides, let her know fear beyond
fear. Let her find her claws and see if she knows what
to do with them. Let her look in the mirror and see a
face with no soul. Let her know nothing, no worth, not
to walk the earth, no right, no reason, let the blood
drip from her mouth, let her bite through the bone, let
her moan, let her whimper, let her kill, let her give no

ground ... revenge ... let her howl. Revenge. Her claws tear the flesh of the face with no soul. Let us see what she is made of. Let her be nothing, a nothing, a nothing, not a thing at all.

Wolverine transforms to Bob,
a successful lawyer,
sitting behind his desk.
Jessica stands frozen,
locked in time,
even though the scene is about to begin.

[CROW *fills in for* JESSICA, *sitting in* The Lawyer's Office, *crossing his legs carefully*]

BOB   Don't get me wrong. I've always thought the halfway house board did the right thing in hiring you. At least the meetings are a lot more exciting since you took over. But I'm still going to resign.

CROW   [*as* JESSICA] Maybe you should try the ballet next time.

BOB   I find I don't have the time for things that are important to me, like my family, and as I'm planning to go into politics, I....

CROW   [*as* JESSICA] You are?

BOB   I can't believe I just told you that, I haven't told anyone....

[JESSICA *takes control and enters* BOB's *office*]

CROW   [*as* JESSICA] I keep getting into trouble, offending everybody....

JESSICA   [*to* CROW] You sure do.

CROW   [*to* JESSICA] I should hire myself out: 'Late for a meeting? Call "Crow, Spirit-guiding with a Difference"....'

JESSICA   If I'm offending anybody, I'll do it myself now.

[JESSICA *changes places with* CROW. BOB *continues as if nothing has happened*]

BOB   There's a difference between dishonesty and diplomacy, if you could learn a little diplomacy, I think things would go easier for you.

JESSICA   They want me to act like someone with their B.A. in social work and I can't.

BOB You mean you won't.

JESSICA I won't.

CROW You mean you can't.

JESSICA [*confused*] I mean I cah.... I wo.... I need your help.

BOB What kind of help?

JESSICA How to talk to Presbyterian bankers, how to handle the publicity we're starting to get, then there's grants, application forms.... I can't even spell, I've got a grade-six education.

BOB You do very well with it.

JESSICA You're the closest thing to a human being I've met in that place.

BOB Thank you, I feel the same way about you.

JESSICA I was hoping you could take me through a few basic tricks, business things ... and then maybe someday I could do something for you.

CROW You've got nothing to offer, it's a bad deal.

BOB It all depends on how far you're willing to go. Often in a certain league there's a necessity for what seems like brutality, but it's usually a clean kill, something expected, even respected. I'm not interested in dealing with innocents or do-gooders.

JESSICA I'm sick of begging, and I'm not afraid of a little blood.

BOB No?

CROW Go for the heart, if you can find it.

JESSICA More and more girls are arriving at the house, in real bad shape, sick, beat up, shot up, you name it, it's like the city's gone wild. They've got nowhere else to go....

CROW Lady H., she is so beautiful....

JESSICA A guy came in the other day who hadn't eaten in a week. When was the last time you didn't eat in a week?

CROW When he was on the Scarsdale diet.

BOB When I was on the Scarsdale diet.... Sorry, but you looked so earnest, I couldn't resist. You see, I don't believe you can change people with these programs. You're different, you got out on your own.

CROW On her own?

JESSICA You remind me of a lot of men I used to know.

BOB Is that good or bad?

JESSICA Neither.

BOB Keep your idealism if you like, but don't waste my time. What you want is a basic night school course.

JESSICA I could make you do it.

BOB How?

JESSICA Let's just say I kept you from moving.

CROW Sign up for that course, or better still, forget the whole thing. Oh, no.

Sharp strings.
Jessica freezes Bob.
Time and space warp.
Crow hides under his wing.
Strobe to Vitaline's kitchen.
Vitaline is sitting with the Unicorn.

VITALINE Jessica! She thinks she's so smart and now he's trapped her. She's gonna be in trouble now.

UNICORN She can't help it. It's the part of her that isn't real. She thinks she doesn't have to play by the rules.

VITALINE Wolverine plays for real.

UNICORN But he's so obvious.

CROW [*to* JESSICA] You better stop now or he might not come back.

Jessica releases Bob.
He has caught a glimpse
of a room and a unicorn.
Bob sinks into a chair,
Jessica is drained.

JESSICA Sorry, I shouldn't have done that.

BOB ...What are you?

JESSICA I'm a ... a sorcerer's apprentice.

BOB Don't play games with me, I don't like it.

CROW Oh, I don't know, I think you like it.

BOB Well, I don't.

JESSICA You're not supposed to use it for yourself, but I could get money, change people's minds, I could help people....

CROW That's what they all say that when they start.

BOB What do you really want from me?

JESSICA Now I just go where it takes me. It took me to you.
BOB What's 'it'?
JESSICA You'd call it magic.
CROW You'd call it bullshit.
BOB There's a lot of bullshit associated with that word.
JESSICA I don't usually do party tricks.
CROW The hell you don't.
BOB The hell you don't.
JESSICA What did you just see?
BOB I saw.... Alright, it's true, I've always been interested in ... in non-ordinary reality, but I can never relate to a crowd that wears crystals on their Birkenstocks.
JESSICA I could teach you.
CROW No you couldn't.
BOB Cream always rises to the top.
JESSICA What does that mean?
BOB You'll see. Are you married?
JESSICA No.
BOB Living with anyone?
JESSICA Nothing serious.
CROW What?
JESSICA There's a board meeting tonight, are you coming?
BOB I think I can arrange it. We should start with two one-hour sessions a week. Mysticism on Tuesdays, corporate behaviour on Thursdays.
JESSICA Thank you. Do we call this friendship?
BOB I'm never friends with attractive women, it always costs too much.

Bob transforms to Wolverine.
The Spirits move quickly in unison.
Jessica enters the apartment,
months later.

[SAM *is sleeping on the apartment couch, he's fallen on bad times.* JESSICA *comes in, wrung out*]
SAM Hey, where've you been, I missed you....
[*He goes to embrace* JESSICA. *She pulls away and starts cleaning up*]
What's the matter with you lately?

JESSICA Nothing.

SAM The kids won't be home for hours, let's do some
wrestling.... It's been a long time....

JESSICA I can't right now.

SAM You mean you don't want to..

JESSICA It's not that.

SAM Just talk to me, I'm not blind, you know....

[JESSICA *starts to fall apart*]

SAM Are you crying again? You're going to dehydrate with
all the crying that's going on....

JESSICA I'm just a bit strange right now, that's all. I'm picking
up on all kinds of things and I'm not used to it....

SAM Every time you come back from seeing that old lady,
you get like this. You start mooning around with this
weird look on your face, the kids don't know who you
are anymore....

JESSICA It's just a stage.

SAM Are you sure? You're using your moods to get things.
You walk into a place looking all weak and pathetic
and people come running....

JESSICA You've got to give me some room.

SAM I've been giving you all kinds of room. The more room
I give you, the more you back away like a scared cat.

JESSICA I never let a man get close before because I was afraid
he'd take something from me.

SAM You've got everything I got to give, there has to be
some taking back in the bargain.

JESSICA It's like there's a place I've got inside that men always
seem to want. Sometimes they don't even want me,
they just want to find out what's in that place, and I
won't let them, I won't let you, I won't let anybody.
It's my secret until I find out what it is....

SAM You like having a secret, it makes you feel special.

JESSICA Yes.

SAM So you're locking me out?

JESSICA I don't want to.

SAM Take what away?

JESSICA I can't put a name on it....

SAM Take what away?

JESSICA My power.

SAM That's where this is all going, I knew it. My uncle was into medicine, I know what it does.... It makes you do numbers on people.... Pretty soon, you're never straight, not for a minute....

JESSICA You don't know what you're talking about.

SAM Pretty soon you'll do anything just to show you can do it.... You're getting it on with that lawyer aren't you?

JESSICA No.

SAM Then come with me and prove it.

JESSICA The thought of it makes me sick.

SAM What's he paying you? Maybe I should fucking leave a hundred bucks under the pillow, and you'd be hanging from the rafters....

JESSICA What would you pay me with, you haven't made a dime in months, you've been living off me, drinking like a pig....

SAM That's not true.

JESSICA What were you doing in that motel room last night? I saw her, you can't hide from me....

SAM You're one of them baby, that's what the lawyer's about and that's what the old lady's about.... You shoot for that high world, that's what you really want, power, any way you can get it.... You're a whore, a good whore, you make them come to you....

JESSICA Strutting around like a big shot, talking up a storm in the bar because you can't make it, tomcatting all over town with anyone that'll have you....

SAM If you're a goddamn whore, let's treat you like a whore....
[SAM grabs JESSICA. He rips open her blouse, revealing a huge purple bruise on her shoulder. She winces]
Where'd you get that bruise?
[She doesn't answer]
Where? So that lawyer beats you up?

JESSICA That's right, because he's a strong man, not a chicken-shit coward, hiding behind my skirts, he beats me up like a man....

SAM [He hits her hard across the face] Shut up.
[JESSICA gets away. SAM comes after her]

You'll do anything to get your way. Well, so will I. You
hear that? So will I....
[*They grapple.* SAM *is raging, but seems to be holding back.*
JESSICA *goes for the balls*]

JESSICA You're a fucking yellow coward, you can't even get it
up ... you're not even half a man....
[SAM *snaps. He punches* JESSICA *in the face. She falls to
the floor, he begins beating her savagely, ending by
punching her full force in the stomach. He finally stops
himself as she screams*]

SAM [*reaches for her*] ... Baby ... you okay? [*She pushes him
away*] I'm sorry babe.... I'm so sorry.... I can't afford to
be gentle, all I know is that when I see red, I fight. It's
too dangerous any other way. You can't ask me why. I
fight. That's what I do. Somehow that's what I'm
supposed to do but it gets all screwed up. There's a
place for it, I know there is, but I don't know where.
You look at me, all bruised up, and you think you're
the one that's hurt, but it's me that's dying. I want to
beat you because I can't beat them, you're just one
step down from me, that's all. You're the one thing
around that's lower than me. You've gotta support
me, you've gotta believe in me, even when I'm an
asshole ... Somewhere in this world I've got to be
right. They did take our balls away, and they hold
them dangling in front of us while we rage around
and try to get them back. All we've got is rage. I can
feel myself switching when I'm strong, feel myself
losing the Bear, he just walks away on me. You've got
your mysteries, all I've got is that sometime I was a
warrior. So I'll get drunk, and sing, and pound the
drum, and dance in the gutter. There's got to be
somebody out there dancing. That's all that's left of
war.

Instantly, Unicorn transforms to Liz.

[LIZ *enters the apartment, loud and breezy*]

LIZ Hey, Jesse, how are you doing? Ooohh, not so good.
[*to* SAM] Did you do this? You're a shit. I'll go get a
cloth.

[LIZ *goes to the kitchen.* SAM *is about to leave*]

JESSICA Don't go away.

SAM You want me to stay?

JESSICA Yes.

SAM You keep switching on me, it's driving me crazy.

JESSICA I know, just don't go away.

SAM I won't.

[LIZ *returns and begins wiping* JESSICA's *face*]

LIZ [*to* SAM] Any self-respecting man goes out and gets drunk after beating up his woman, and you're going to sit there and watch me clean her up?

SAM That's right.

LIZ Well, at least have a beer or something, it doesn't look right.

SAM Jesus. [*He goes for a beer*]

LIZ [*to* JESSICA] Did you ask for it?

JESSICA Sort of....

LIZ It's better that way. I've been hearing all kinds of stories about you....

JESSICA There's always a million bar stories.

LIZ Like you're trying to turn into a Black Panther, but at the same time you're runnning around with some high-class lawyer who's also a do-gooder, you've got a house for women too stupid to make it on their own, and you're studying to be a witch.

JESSICA Doesn't sound like a bad life.

[*They laugh a bit*]

Ouch! I'm getting into a lot of trouble trying to get some money together for the movement....

[SAM *enters with a beer*]

LIZ The only movement those guys know about is on the toilet seat with their pants down. Right Sam?

SAM That's right.

LIZ At least he's steady. What about the witch business?

[JESSICA *doesn't answer*]

SAM That's all you'll get out of her.

JESSICA I don't talk about it because you don't like me to.

SAM That's not why. I'm not some dumb guy you can treat like a personal bouncer. Lots of muscle and warm at night, but don't give him the inside story.

JESSICA Okay, we have ceremonies, sometimes in the sweat
 lodge. The spirits come, they talk....
 LIZ But what does it feel like?
JESSICA It ... tingles.
 SAM Tingles?
 LIZ Does it tingle where I think it tingles?
JESSICA There's nothing like it. When I feel them, and I'm not
 scared out of my mind, it's the highest I've ever been.
 LIZ Like ... a hit?
JESSICA Like fishing. You feel the hook, it's got you right in the
 pit of your stomach, and the spirits are on the other
 end. They pull you, and you pull them, and sometimes
 they let everything go slack so you can wonder for a
 while. You know you could tear away but you don't
 want to because you're only sure of one thing, that
 there's something on the other end.
 SAM How much do you believe?
JESSICA Most of it ... all of it ... I don't know.
 SAM No doubts?
JESSICA Of course. I used to be terrible, Vitaline'd get so mad.
 I'd be checking the sweat lodge for tape recorders and
 secret entrances. She'd say I was too modern, too
 white....
 SAM Maybe you are.
JESSICA But they love me, I know they do.
 LIZ Can I come sometime, maybe get high with you?

 Dark, languid music.
 Wolverine moves slowly
 toward the apartment.
 Wolverine transforms to Bob.

JESSICA I keep pushing it, I just keep pushing it....
 LIZ [*fishing a mickey out her purse*] You need a shot, have
 some of this, beer's for the poor.
JESSICA I'm not supposed to drink....
 LIZ One shot won't hurt you....
JESSICA What the hell. [*takes a swig of whisky*]
 [BOB *enters the apartment. He is upset, surprisingly*
 vulnerable]

BOB   Jessica? Sorry to bother you, I just came by.... [*sees her face*] What happened?

SAM   I don't think we've met.

JESSICA   Sam, this is Bob Wainright.

SAM   Yessir, about time we met.

LIZ   Jesse?

JESSICA   Sorry, Liz. This is Bob.

LIZ   You must be the laywer. I could tell by the cut of your suit. You're pretty cute ... are you married? You know what we were talking about? Beating up women ... Do you beat up your wife?

BOB   Ahh, no, no I don't.

LIZ   What do you do then?

BOB   We use other kinds of warfare.

SAM   I bet.

BOB   Jessica, could I speak to you for a minute?

LIZ   You know what this cabinet minister used to like?

BOB   I'll bite, what?

LIZ   He used to like walking around on his hands and knees with a peacock feather shoved up his ass while someone in a black garter belt beat him with a rolled up newspaper singing, 'Dirty birdie, dirty birdie'.... What do you like?

BOB   Jesse?

JESSICA   You look a little shook up, what is it? Did we get turned down?

BOB   I'd like to talk to you alone.

SAM   I'm not leaving.

LIZ   If Sam's not going, I'm not going.

JESSICA   I'll come round to the office tomorrow.

BOB   It can't wait, some pretty weird things are happening....

LIZ   They sure are.

BOB   I can't speak here....

SAM   Go ahead, you've got nothing to lose....

BOB   I've never known that to be true.

JESSICA   Go ahead, I think I know....

BOB   Are you alright? It would just take one phone call....

SAM   Nothing takes one phone call.

LIZ We won't say a word, right Sam?
[*as* BOB *and* JESSICA *speak, their voices overlap*]

BOB It's just that I had an odd experience driving home last night / ... I was driving along this road, it was very dark....

JESSICA I had a dream last night / ....

BOB And I see this thing, this wolf or cat or something / I don't know....

JESSICA Sometimes I feel like I have to run / I can't stop myself, I just have to go....

BOB An animal or cat, like a feline thing / and it's running beside the car....

JESSICA Last night I dreamt I was running, and I looked down and saw two / front paws....

BOB And I get to a stop sign / ....

JESSICA There's something incredible stretching out that far / something a two-legged never feels....

BOB So I slow down to a stop and it looks at me ... it was you / ....

JESSICA I was running to get away from / something....

BOB I mean it was still an animal / but the face was yours....

JESSICA It was very real / I could feel it right down inside.

BOB When I start up the car / it runs alongside again....

JESSICA Then I ran across the road....

BOB Then it runs in front of me....

JESSICA Something big and black / with eyes that blinded me....

BOB And I hit the damn thing....

JESSICA I could feel myself being hit / ... I dragged myself off the road....

BOB I thought I'd killed it, I hit it that hard....

JESSICA It hurt so much / I didn't understand....

BOB I ran out, and there was nothing there, not a thing ... gone, no blood ... nothing....

JESSICA When I woke up I had this.
[JESSICA *opens her blouse and shows the bruise*]

BOB My car has five hundred dollars worth of body damage....

JESSICA Sorry.

LIZ I don't think the insurance company would go for that explanation.

SAM [*to* JESSICA] You're saying that's how it happened?

JESSICA I didn't know what to tell you....

SAM But you knew how to turn me into an ape.

BOB That wouldn't take a lot of work.

SAM You're not going to get her that way.

BOB When I see what you did to her, I just can't.... If she gave me a nod, I'd have her out of here in a second.

SAM Don't be so holy, she's got two bruises, man, and they're not both from me.

JESSICA Just cool it, Bob....

LIZ No, keep on going, Bob, you're great....

BOB [*to* JESSICA] I love you.

LIZ Wow....

SAM This is my place, and you've got no respect, so you're getting thrown out....

BOB [*to Jessica*] As they say in the business, the offer still stands.

SAM As they say in the business, you are an asshole.

[JESSICA *sways, as if going to pass out*]

Jesse, you okay?

JESSICA [*disembodied*] Sometimes I feel like I could kill you, not just you, but me and the kids too. I'd like to use a knife, but maybe I'd just give them sleeping pills mixed with milk. I'd carry them into the kitchen ... watch them trying to breathe. Then maybe I'd use a knife on them, on me, or a gun.... I wouldn't kill you, but I would kill you, because I'd make sure you found us, lined up like that.... She's standing over there.

LIZ Who?

JESSICA She's got a face with no soul.

Strobe blackout.
Chaotic sound.
Bob transforms to Wolverine.
Hours pass.

[*Lights up on* VITALINE'*s kitchen.* SAM *and* VITALINE *are in the middle of an old argument*]

SAM You can't make praying the answer to everything, everybody turns into a fluffball and doesn't do anything.

VITALINE There's nothing fluffy about the spirits.

SAM There's got to be action.

VITALINE That's your job, you're a man.

SAM Then I'm doing my job.

VITALINE But you can't do your job unless women are doing their job.

SAM There's nothing wrong with women.

VITALINE They're too busy acting like they're powerful, without looking at the mother, the grandmother, the female power.

SAM Everytime they do that, they start crying.

VITALINE Then you wait for them to stop.

SAM I'm talking about revolution.

VITALINE I'm talking about revolution. The spirits aren't against fighting, they're against losing.

SAM You've got a mind like a highway, it only goes in straight lines.

VITALINE This mind goes in circles and don't you forget it.

SAM You're teaching her to hate me.

VITALINE You want a woman to love you, or a slave?

Jessica stands in
the cabin doorway,
stalked by
Wolverine, whispering.

JESSICA Vitaline, you've got to help me ...

WOLVERINE You are nothing, see nothing, understand nothing ...

JESSICA Sam, you shouldn't see this.

WOLVERINE So many enemies, all to get back, track them down, get them back, make them pay, any way you can....

JESSICA Vitaline, you've got to help me.

SAM Look at her, you're driving her out of her mind, she'll be nuts again, just like when I found her.

VITALINE Maybe, maybe not.

SAM Are you trying to kill her?

VITALINE You have to be willing to risk everything.

SAM Then your power has a death wish. I feel power. It

	comes when the sun shines in the morning and I feel good. I take the world step by step until I get somewhere.
VITALINE	And how do you feel when it's dark?
	[WOLVERINE *shadows* JESSICA]
WOLVERINE	The wrong kind of power, useless egos going nowhere....
	[VITALINE *protects* WOLVERINE]
VITALINE	[*to* SAM] She's got to go to her dark side, so if you want to stick around, you'd better sit tight.
SAM	Oh no you don't. I'm leaving and taking her with me.
WOLVERINE	You want to go with that? You can get better than that, there are so many others who want you.
SAM	Jesse?
VITALINE	She can't leave now.
JESSICA	Let go of me.
WOLVERINE	No.
SAM	Jesse?
VITALINE	[*to* SAM] Don't let her touch you.
SAM	[*to* JESSICA] I love you.
WOLVERINE	Three little words. [*pushes* JESSICA *away*] Go with him then.
SAM	In the old days, medicine women were still partners for their men.
VITALINE	And the men knew enough to help them.
SAM	I am helping her.
JESSICA	I am a partner for a man.
SAM	Not for this man.
VITALINE	[*to* SAM] You watch that Wolverine.
JESSICA	[*to* SAM] Don't leave me.
SAM	You're making me leave you.
JESSICA	[*switching to Wolverine*] Then maybe I'll just piss all over your famous bed.
WOLVERINE	No partners....
JESSICA	There are no partners....
WOLVERINE / JESSICA	Only one who gives and one who takes, he'll never....
JESSICA	Let you be on top ... he'll be jealous....
WOLVERINE	He'll squash you flat ...

VITALINE [*to Sam*] Don't listen to her now. Just try to let her in.... There's a whole side you have to accept. She has to let the Wolverine inside, something wild that could save you both.

[UNICORN *and* CROW *move in*]

SAM [*to* VITALINE] You're the Wolverine, you're ripping us apart so you can have her and keep her with you.... Get in the car, Jesse.

JESSICA Get in the car, Jesse.

WOlVERINE / JESSICA What's he got to offer?

SAM Nothing much, just a chance not to be one of those ladies with pointy hats living alone in the bush....

JESSICA Alone?

SAM Alone.

JESSICA I don't want to be alone.

VITALINE You don't have to be alone.

SAM Oh no? Where's your husband, out chopping wood?

VITALINE Touche.

SAM You want to divide us up, build a wall, and that's how they get us every time. Everybody goes into their corners to get pissed off. We have to be on the same goddamn side. It's men and women on the bottom against the Beast who's going to push the button. And if we don't fight that, there isn't going to be any praying to any spirits, dark side, light side, any side.

VITALINE And what about that Beast? Eh? How did that Beast get born? [VITALINE *waves her cane, in a full state of power*] Thousands of years ago, there was a balance between the Sun and the Moon, then a crack opened up, a crack like the middle of an old lady's ass. And from that crack came that Beast.

[WOLVERINE *crawls to* SAM]

WOLVERINE And the Beast said to the Sun, 'Aren't you tired of all those shadows and mysteries? All those women running around in their underwear? They're laughing at you. You could crush them if you wanted. Wouldn't it be nice if there was only one kind of light?'

[UNICORN *moves to* JESSICA]

UNICORN And the Beast said to the Moon, 'Think of him, he

needs you so much, you have so much to give.... Give in to him, after all, he isn't very bright. Hide your shining for a while. Hate him in secret. A little sacrifice, there's so much glory in sacrifice.'

VITALINE He took, and she gave and gave until there was nothing left but migraine headaches and sacrifice. The Sun shone all day and all night. The Moon hid behind clouds, betraying her own light. The balance was broken. The whole earth has to do with that balance, the tides and the winds and the growth of everything. Nothing can be right again without it, nothing.
[JESSICA *breaks away*]

JESSICA I don't want to be alone. I don't want to wake up alone and go to sleep alone. I don't want to pretend my pillow is a lover.

SAM Does that mean you want me, or just anybody?

WOLVERINE It means any pair of arms will do.

SAM You don't love me, do you?
[JESSICA, *unable to speak, tries to focus on* SAM]

WOLVERINE How can a woman lost in shadows love anyone?
[SAM *and* JESSICA *desperately reach out to each other*]

SAM Jesse?

JESSICA Yes I do....

SAM Do what?

JESSICA I do ... lo ... that's all....

SAM Can't you say it? You've said it before.

WOLVERINE She was lying, covering her tracks....

SAM [*backs away*] I've got to go....

JESSICA Yeah, you have to get out of here.
[SAM *turns to leave*]
No, wait!

WOLVERINE Just like a woman.

JESSICA Wait for me....

SAM For how long?

WOLVERINE Don't wait five minutes.

VITALINE Jessica! Let him go.

SAM I'll wait as long as I can, that's all I can say. I am a warrior. I have courage and honour and love. [*to* VITALINE] You protect her or I'll smash your face.

[SAM *leaves*]

VITALINE That wasn't bad. No, I'll say that was pretty good.

Flute.
Slowly, Jessica turns to face
Wolverine, who kisses her.
She slumps to the floor.
Wolverine transforms to Bob.
Jessica transforms to Wolverine.

[BOB *enters the office.* JESSICA / WOLVERINE *rises,*
turning on VITALINE]

JESSICA / WOLVERINE Vitaline, trying to save the world, she
finds the student, someone to pass it on, connect up
the loose threads, someone to heal poor mother earth.
Don't you hear her? She's dying, she's howling, you
can't pray to her anymore, it's time for revenge....

VITALINE That's not the only way....

JESSICA / WOLVERINE You need to believe, and I'll piss and foul
your belief.

VITALINE What about Jesse? What about her power?

JESSICA / WOLVERINE I'll steal it.

VITALINE How?

JESSICA / WOLVERINE You'll give it to me.

VITALINE I don't think I could do that.

JESSICA / WOLVERINE [*cringing and wringing her hands*] Ohhh,
I'm sorry, I didn't mean it, just give me a little bit, just
a little bit will do....

VITALINE [*drained*] You make me tired.

JESSICA / WOLVERINE Do I?

VITALINE [*grabbing* JESSICA] Not that tired. Jesse? You hear me.
This is what you were afraid of, and now you're in the
middle. It's just you, a part of you. You're strong
enough to take that Wolverine, he's the last one, Jesse,
the last one.

JESSICA / WOLVERINE She's lost, and it's all your fault.

[JESSICA / WOLVERINE *moves deliberately toward the*
office. The SPIRITS *gather close.* BOB *sits at his desk.*
JESSICA / WOLVERINE *enters the office*]

BOB Jessica? The cheque came in.

JESSICA / WOLVERINE What cheque?

    BOB Five months of filling out forms and you don't
        remember what cheque?

JESSICA / WOLVERINE The one for the House and the
        Association?

    BOB It's for a hundred thousand dollars.

JESSICA / WOLVERINE I want it.

    BOB You mean personally?

JESSICA / WOLVERINE Power is a commodity. Cream always
        rises to the top. Money is power. Idealists get bitter.
        Isn't that what you said?

    BOB I don't want to see you anymore.

JESSICA / WOLVERINE You think I've changed.

    BOB You've learned too well. All that sexy idealism is
        gone. Now you're just like me.

JESSICA / WOLVERINE That's right, and it's all your fault.

    BOB But it's been a bad deal. I've risked my family, my
        standing in the community. What have you risked?
        I've taught you, but you haven't taught me anything.

JESSICA / WOLVERINE You said you loved me.

    BOB You're capable of certain kinds of illusion, slightly
        more skilled than a two-bit tart giving blow jobs in a
        parking lot. As far as I can tell you have no real
        spiritual life, I don't think you'd know a spirit if you
        fell over one.

JESSICA / WOLVERINE Don't say those things.

    BOB You're an opportunist using the suffering of your
        people for personal gain. I'm going to cut my losses
        now, and return to what has always been a very nice
        life.

JESSICA / WOLVERINE [*the unbalanced* WOLVERINE *begins to take
        over*] You want me to forget, you want me to ignore....
        Are you sorry? Please don't be sorry. I can't hurt you,
        I have no guard.... Oh please protect me ... and give it
        to me, give it to me. They're laughing at you, at the
        failure that you are.

    BOB I'm ... not afraid of you.

JESSICA / WOLVERINE You walk into the bank and your accounts
        are all empty. They don't know who you are. The
        police come and throw you in the street. All lost, all

lost. Your wife's fucking your partner, they're
laughing at you, going through your precious things,
all your money, all your power. All lost, the future
failed, the past failed. Failure on your face, your
fingers, failure on your cock, it won't rise, not ever
again. No house, no clothes, no land, no car.... Your
children are laughing at you, they hate weakness, it
makes them sick. You try to walk with your head up,
whimpering to yourself, hands shaking, smelling of
dead flesh, and shhhhhhhshhhsttttttt! On your face in
the shit. With all of your courage, you drag yourself to
your feet, you think you've gotten away with it and
then ... haughhghghghhghstttt! And when you rest,
panting in the gutter, pissing yourself in fright, you
find a final bit of strength, and slowly slowly crawl to
your knees, back uncoiling, and at that moment, when
you stand clean, face to the sun ...
auuuuuughhhhhaahhhhhhhgggh!
[BOB *is down on the floor, and* JESSICA's *hands are around*
his neck. He is choking, getting weaker]

JESSICA / WOLVERINE Nothing to trust. Your songless throat
closes with no chance for a prayer, they've been
ripped from your chest, regret is like smoke, you
breathe it in and it never goes away.... You've stolen
the breath from yourself, you've stolen the breath
from yourself....
[JESSICA / WOLVERINE *breaks away, remembering the*
ceremony] I'm not standing in a fertile place, I'm
standing in a place that's dry and empty, like a
desert....
[VITALINE *moves silently to the ceremony circle.* BOB *gets*
to his feet, gasping]

BOB You almost killed me.... Don't sell me short. I saw my
life pass before me.... Maybe you are worth it.... All
this talk about visions ... I finally saw something.

JESSICA / WOLVERINE What did you see?

BOB [*softly*] The Wolverine.

Vitaline's chant cuts the air.
Jessica is propelled toward her.

Vitaline catches her.
Bob transforms to Wolverine.
The ceremony returns
full circle.

[JESSICA *and* VITALINE *return to their positions at the*
beginning of the ceremony]

VITALINE I humbly ask you to help her enter the circle in her
own way.

JESSICA It's as if there's a stone in there, and unless I let it
loose, I'm going to die.

VITALINE Jesse? Where's Wolverine?

JESSICA Inside.

[WOLVERINE *leaves the ceremony*]

CROW Where's Crow?

[JESSICA *turns to* CROW. *They exchange a long look.*
CROW *leaves the ceremony*]

VITALINE And Coyote?

JESSICA Vitaline?

[VITALINE *walks out of the circle*]

BEAR How about Bear?

JESSICA Sam?

[BEAR *leaves the ceremony*]

UNICORN Where's Unicorn, Jesse?

[JESSICA *pauses a moment, then opens her hands, palms*
up, and balances them. UNICORN *leaves the ceremony*]

VITALINE What do you see?

JESSICA I don't know. Someone made of smoke, maybe it's a
man, maybe it's a woman.

VITALINE Look closer.

JESSICA It's like we've conjured her up, and she can't quite get
through.

VITALINE Who is she?

JESSICA I don't want to look at her....

VITALINE Who is she? Name her.

JESSICA I feel like I'm drowning....

VITALINE Keep breathing....

JESSICA She's bigger than she should be, I don't want her to be
that big....

VITALINE Name her.

JESSICA She doesn't have a name.
VITALINE What's her name?
JESSICA Nothing.
VITALINE Grandmothers and grandfathers, give me strength!
Call her now or you'll never see her again. Name her.
JESSICA Jessica!
[JESSICA *throws back her head. Small sounds escape from
her throat. The sounds lengthen as she births them.
Extending and weaving, a melody emerges, searching for a
peak. We breathe with her until her call bursts through,
triumphant*]
[*Blackout*]

Editors for the Press:
David Young and Robert Wallace

For a list of our drama and other titles,
or to receive a catalogue, write to

The Coach House Press
401 (rear) Huron Street
Toronto, Canada M5S 2G5
(416) 979-7374.